1

"God, pour yourself into me and utilize me for a greater higher purpose than myself"
~*Richard Seaman*

"You are here for a reason. How I believe you master your life is to understand that you are co-creating your life with the ultimate creator. Not understanding this puts you at your own pitiful, meager little will and everything is left up to you. You cannot do it; you cannot survive in this world by yourself just believing in yourself. You are not big enough to do it alone, I am not big enough to do it, no one is big enough to do it alone. You have to understand that your very presence here as a human being on earth came from something greater than yourself and not just your parents who wanted to have a child, the fact that egg was hit by that particular sperm in that particular moment and you were created should blow you away. Wow – how amazing is that?"

~ Oprah Winfrey

Spiritual Reliability

Learning to Become God's Employee

Richard Seaman

www.SeattleLifeCoachTraining.com

Table of Contents

Foreword

Don't dim my light! That was the warning Richard Seaman gave me as one of his employers here on earth several years ago. This affirmation was not in the least way said in a threatening or condescending manner; Richard was just very aware that his fulltime employer was God. Often without warning some amazing force would show up and come out his mouth . . . sometimes with grace, other times with real raw honesty. Before long it became increasingly obvious Richard was on loan as an employee to the college and that his real job was to be a *spirit-directed pot-stirrer.* He was in our employ to shake things up, do things a little differently and to prepare for his next assignment.

Richard has been very reliable in showing up to deeply touch the lives of many people, to help heal their stories in a very real way, and help to free many souls. There is no doubt this new book is his continued commitment to serve as a teacher and guide for those who are ready to do their own work in recovering and discovering.

As the founder and director of an award-winning private college dedicated to inspiring people to discover their gifts and graces, there have been hundreds of employees who have helped to serve thousands of students over the years. As an employer it is my job to learn to manage the thoroughbreds like Richard. I cannot hope to tame them; it is my job to help contain their brilliance until they are ready to go out in to the world again on their own in a loving and profitable way. I have long ago come to realize employees are a lot like children you are asked to raise; you pour many resources into their care and feeding, you spend many hours nurturing and holding their fears and concerns only to have them pack their bags one day to follow the call of destiny. It's bittersweet.

Richard did just that when he left the security of Arizona and Southwest Institute of Healing Arts to start Seattle Life Coach Training. Richard took with him two awards he received: *The Lighthouse Award* given by the college acknowledging the leadership and light he provided to the staff and students, and the *Best Teacher of the Year* award from the Arizona Private School Association for his educational excellence in and out of the classroom.

It was interesting to note the logo Richard chose for his new venture in Seattle was a lighthouse. It was not until after the new logo was designed and implemented did he remember the award he won. Somewhere deep within him was a knowing of God's greater plan. Whether this new book wins any earthly awards or not is not as important as the fact that Richard has done the work that would win an award from the employer that ultimately counts—**God**.

Truth be known, we all have a sacred employment contract with the Divine. Part of

Richard's definition of *Spiritual Reliability* is the act of showing up for a greater, higher purpose, willing to go forth even when you cannot see the entire path beneath your feet. By this definition, as well as the feeling deep in my heart, there is no question Richard Seaman has been hired by the Divine to be a powerful instrument of the light. **No one will dim this man's light!**

Blessings,

KC Miller
Founder of Southwest Institute of Healing Arts

Preface

You're probably wondering what does being spiritually reliable mean anyway?

Spiritual Reliability means being loyal and obedient to the truth of spirit as it arrives in each moment.

As I began writing *Spiritual Reliability*, I was forced to look at my own reliability in regard to my life and this book. I started this project with an intention to write a book, which is different from the earlier book I wrote, *It's All in the Sharing*. I didn't become reliable to *Sharing* until it was in its final stages. With *Sharing*, I didn't set out to write a book; it was a personal journal that birthed itself in a strange way and became a book. It happened suddenly, when I somehow realized it was a book and that I needed to publish it. This time is different because I set out to write a book, which means I have to be spiritually reliable and commit to its final outcome. I have to show up like it is a job that I have been hired to do. I realize that God is my employer, and like any successful employer, God needs good employees.

Many people seek counsel from me in my private coaching practice. A large number of people want to find their purpose in life. Usually, the first question out of my mouth is:

If God were an employer, would he hire you?

If you find yourself struggling to answer this question, my invitation to you is to see this book you are reading now as a vessel for you to grow, evolve and Up-Level everything in your life! Just like an employer who has hired you to do a job, God will send you out into the world to serve, but only if you are spiritually reliable and 100% committed to the job. He prefers to send out those who are consistent and live their lives with follow through, integrity and will show up with a positive and activated attitude. If you are floundering to answer this question there may be some up leveling that needs to be dealt with in your life.

Most people in this world wish to live a life

that is purposeful, while also having the greatest intentions of helping the world and making it a better place. I once heard someone say that many spiritual people have taken on a belief that you are going to be broke if you are spiritual. This belief needs to be shattered. The reality is that we live in a western world, which means that we have bills, rent, food and finances to meet in order to survive. We're not mystics in a monastery; we are mystics in the world. So as a result we must learn to monetize our skills, gifts and talents. You will be compensated financially to the same degree that you add value into the world.

If you believe, like millions of other people in the world, that you do not have a life purpose, you are cheating yourself. That belief in and of itself is denying your purpose from manifesting. You need to reframe these thoughts. I have five questions for you to ponder as you read this book that could increase your potential of doing so.

1) What is your gift to the world?
2) What is your message to share with the world?
3) What can you teach?
4) How can you inspire and shine a light into the world?
5) How can you bring a piece of truth to someone's life?

Usually, what I have found is that

wherever you have had to *do the biggest piece of work* in your life is where you will be the most powerful. I sometimes say, "Your mess becomes your ministry; your messes become your message."

My teachings convey how to be spiritually reliable. Like all people, I struggle with being spiritually reliable at times, but I always go back to a teaching that has enlightened me.

We teach what we need to learn the most.

Sometimes it is not easy to show up for God and be his instrument. Other times it can be very easy to show up because there is a groove we slide into. It somehow lifts us up, over and through the struggle, ultimately connecting to God to become *spirits'* tool. This space of possibility is a mystery to me every day. Why can we sometimes find the "groove" and why do we lose it at other times?

God is the ultimate all-knowing divine being, moving through you and all around you. You are always supported by God's presence; therefore, you are never disconnected from God. Why do we waver in this reality if this is true? Why do we feel disconnected from God?

This book is about recognizing and learning how to become spiritually reliable, allowing you to be utilized for God's greater, higher purpose. This book is going to give you practical spiritual tools and skills to apply in your everyday life, giving you a grounded, solid foundation from which to work. These tools will create your new normal if you apply them consistently for the next three to six months.

I have been a Life Coach and teacher for fifteen years. Thousands of people have shared their life stories with me and I have figured out why so many of us suffer in our lives. It is because we feel we are disconnected from others, and therefore, disconnected from God, which leads us to believe that God doesn't love us. Most of us were never introduced to God as an all-loving presence who supports us. Most of us were born and raised into families that believe God is judgmental and punishes us when we are bad. Many of us disconnect from this fierce God who will send us to hell. We are all sinners according to religion.

It doesn't surprise me that our world has become so unhealthy and dysfunctional when most of us have disconnected from the ultimate power. This power can keep us grounded and aligned to our greatness and goodness while keeping us in the light. Religion has failed the world and given humanity a vein of fear, which manipulates our sense of self-righteousness and teaches us judgment and separation. If there is sin, the *Course of Miracles* says, "Sin could be defined as the perception we are separated from self and/or we are separated from our Creator."[1]

The truth is we are always connected and always being supported by our Higher Power.

When Jesus walked the earth he didn't teach fear, lack or separateness. He taught the nine fruits of the Spirit: Love, Joy, Peace, Patience, Kindness, Goodness, Faithfulness, Gentleness and Self-Control. Against such things there is no law.[2]

When I see these four letters, "WWJD" (What would Jesus do?) It reminds me and aligns me with the mind of Jesus.

There are many other teachers, past and present, who have taken on this compassion towards humanity to aid in the greater good of the world. Teachers like: Mother Theresa, Gandhi, Don Miguel Ruiz, Wayne Dyer, Marianne Williamson, Buddha, Deepak Chopra, Caroline Myss, Oprah Winfrey, Neale Donald Walsch, Joel Osteen and many more. The theme within these great teachers is that they are *spiritually reliable*. They are willing to be utilized for a greater higher purpose. They asked the question, "How may I best serve?" They listened, and then acted with their life to contribute to a greater, more profound, healing purpose in the world.

I am here to teach you a spiritual way that will empower you to know yourself and God in dynamic ways, and when you think of God you will be open to receive all the abundance He has for your life. May you know there is enough for everyone; and that digging in the garbage for sustenance is not necessary, nor is it part of the plan for you. Know there is always enough and God is supporting you all the time.

This book is for anyone who walked away from God because of religious constraints, boxes and judgments. This book is about connecting and reconnecting you to your spirituality, which is available to everyone if you just open up and move towards it; it is about connecting you to the art of "spiritual reliability," returning you back to the presence of love, coming home to the ultimate power of the Universe and helping you recover from religion.

There is religion and there is spirituality. The differences between the two are profound, yet similar. I am not here to judge religion, but to shine a light to guide you back, if you've ever left or departed, because of the disconnection you may have experienced through religion.

Each person has their own timeline and will experience their "Awe Ha's" in perfect, divine timing. God is perfectly on time and never late.

You have a lot to share with the world. It is now time to show up for your self, and God will take care of the details. There are no random accidents; therefore, you have a divine appointment with this book.

"Dear God, Please melt the walls that separate me from others, imprisoning me within myself. Please heal my wounded places and free my heart to love. Help me connect to others that I might isolate no more. I know, dear God, that when I am alone, I fear; and when I fear, I self-destruct. What I suffer now and I have suffered

before, Dear God, may I suffer no more. And, so it is."

Spiritually Reliable~
R.R.Seaman

Acknowledgments

I often wonder where would I be if I had not listened to God's voice. Where would I be if I had not stepped onto the path to walk a Spiritually Reliable life?

I remember a time when I had one of those break down moments in the shower. I felt as if I was losing my mind, losing parts and pieces of myself. I cried out so loud to God, "I know I am amazing, talented and fabulous. I know I am not here to sling pasta in an Italian restaurant for the rest of my life. I am ripe and ready for the picking—God use me as your Divine instrument, in the peace and healing of others. God, I cannot go on anymore like this. I beg you, PLEASE send someone to produce me!"

It was a desperate attempt to get Gods attention, which, in my case is never anything short of melodramatic. I had gone complacent and was walking around in my life going through the motions, having temporary, fleeting in-sights—dreaming and seeing who I could become. Standing naked in the shower, water dripping down my body seemed metaphorical as I was having an emotional crisis, screaming, crying and complaining of how things were not working in my life. Then I heard the Voice—the voice neither male nor female, a voice so clear, direct, and precise like a laser, surround me from all directions and yell into me—**Produce Yourself**!

Yes, I thought, "Yes," I screamed out loud back at the Voice. "Is that what you want? You want me to show up, move my feet and produce myself? Then show me the way, show me how, open doors and I will walk through them all." I yelled. From this Holy Instant, this Holy break-through the doors did open, and quite rapidly I must add, and my life was never the same again.

Since, saying Yes to my Divine destiny, God's love has manifested in my life as a massive amount of unconditional love. This love has appeared in a multitude of layers from people, places and events in my life. Each one being colored in miracles beyond my wildest dreams.

Thank you God for Yelling into me, *Produce Yourself* as this book is now one of the many physical manifestations to the many Yeses I spoke back to you when you gave me my divine orders. I said Yes to being an awarding winning, global, world wide speaker, writer and teacher many years ago and this has manifested as my reality. I thank you for trusting me with this magical calling and life purpose, and for this truth, I thank you God for the grace you have bestowed upon me. I am honored to do your work on earth, as it is done in heaven, to the best of my human-abilities.

I have learned four BIG lessons since I began to show up and produce myself.

1) The Divine plan for your life is never a straight shot to the goal.

2) When you think you know the plan, be prepared to shift with Spirit's needs. A Spiritually Reliable person is able to reset and readjust quickly!

3) Let go of the When, Where and How. All you need to do is say Yes to being a vessel for the peace and healing of others and let the Universe work out all the details.

4) God can dream a bigger dream than you can dream for yourself. When you let go and let God, what shows up as your divine compensation is remarkable and beyond your wildest dreams.

To my mother, Sandra Seaman, who lost her life during the creation of this book, your untimely, confusing departure rocked my world and left a giant hole in my body. The intense pain and anxiety I once felt has lessened and been replaced with a deep knowing your work on earth was done. The spiritual lessons I received from your earthwork and now your divine eye in the sky position, far surpasses any human-pain I may experience from time to time. It was your death that taught me about spiritual lessons and was the catalyst that gave me the perspective to write the chapter *Spiritual Lessons* in this book. I carry you with me daily, and only need to close my eyes for a visit or look into the eyes of your sisters to see you.

To my father, Ron Seaman, you taught me how to be a reliable, hardworking, trustworthy, respectful person in the world. Your ground training was the foundation from which my Spiritually Reliable nature was born. You are a man of your word and walk a Spiritually Reliable life, even if you do not know this about yourself— it's true.

KC Miller, who I refer to as the "touch and go" lady. You do go and you go fast, like the speed of light, which is what it takes to touch as many lives as you do. You never hang out too long in any one place because you are in constant conversation with GUS and as we both know, when you work for God, Universe, Spirit, free-will takes on a whole new meaning. You are the epitome of someone who is a true spiritual listener and one who really does walk a real *Spiritually Reliable life*. Thank you for seeing my gifts and graces and supporting me as I take them into the world in a loving and profitable way.

Michelle Medrano, minster from New Vision Spiritual Center in Scottsdale, AZ. As you grew up in your ministry, I grew up in your Sunday services. Each message became a part of this book. You are a dynamic, bold, passionate and highly spiritual being who knows how to share your spiritual wisdom in a compelling powerful, graceful way.

Phoenix, AZ you have this interesting way of pulling people who are dying spiritual deaths into your clutches, shedding and releasing all those things which are no longer serving them. I refer to you has the place that people go to burn off their "personal garbage," and once you've burned us to our inner cores, smoldering and seared, we rise from the ashes and take our new found selves into the world more whole and complete than when we arrived in your fire. I thank you for the fire you burned into me for the last decade I laid in your divine clutches.

To Pedro Ochoa, your unconditional all-inclusive way of being is what I admire in you the most. Your constant loyal companionship and your contagious, youthful joy ground me and bring me much inner joy. Each time I would birth a new chapter I would drag you into my office for the preview—the time we spent developing was remarkably helpful.

Sherra Grasser, you know we had a divine appointment. God hired you many years ago and I was just the human who gave you the job. You lift me up, hold the pieces, take what I cannot and up-level the inner workings and systems of SLCT in Seattle. You are truly Spiritually Reliable and I am so happy we found each other in this big world.

Linda Bennett, Jenny Gwinn McGlothern, Brandie Smith, Christina Giordano, Carmen Marrero, Rob Austin, Kelly Harrison, Lesley Pelkey, Carla Crujido, Amber Borgomainerio, and Aandra Bohlen you are all held in a very special place within my heart. We both know how we connect and what our unique relationship brings to us. You all make me more complete and I feel connected, loved and supported by you— Thank you.

Sharon Cusack and Ally Pisher, I thank you for stepping up as Spiritually Reliable mid-wife's birthing this book into the world. You both supported the flow and forward movement it took to place this manuscript into the hands of the many readers it will touch in the world.

Roberta Huffer you were the first spark that lit a fire under me to start writing this book and of course as divine order would have it, you were one of the last people to read it cover to cover, tuning it up before the world got it.

Krista Burlae you and I had a divine appointment and I feel my invitation for you to edit this book was something you needed as much as I needed it from you. I was bombarded by many to professionally edit, but when I found you those God bumps spoke loud and clear you were the one—Thank you.

Lastly, I am grateful to my students wherever, you may be in the world. My work is a collective consciousness between the Divine— You and Me. Without all three present in the equation, which represents the holy trinity, I do not believe any of this information would have ever been put into the physical form. You are all seekers of the truth and your willingness to show up in my classroom for 100-Hours or more is beyond Spiritually Reliable. We all knew that something bigger was going on in those classes than just another class. Each of you rose up and gave me a view into your life, your fears, struggles and passions. You shared your vulnerabilities and secrets, and through it all you found courage, passion, purpose and left with a plan. I hold you all in a very special place in my heart—Thank you.

One Power

There's One Power, invisible, and you see it
everywhere and every day.
There's One Power, indescribable, and you
speak of it in every word you say.
Mysterious until you know the truth.
As simple as the love inside of you.

Call it God, call it Spirit, call it Jesus, call it Lord,
call it Buddha, Bahá'u'lláh, angel's wings or
Heaven's door, but whatever name you give it,
it's all One Power, can't you see? It's the power
of the love in you and me.

We speak so many languages, have different
clothing, different colors, different names, but
different is only dangerous when we forget that
in the heart we're all the same. And we'll
remember when we close our eyes to see
that such distances and separations were never
meant to be.

Call it God, call it Spirit, call it Jesus, call it Lord,
call it Buddha, Bahá'u'lláh, Angel's Wings or
Heaven's Door. It's Muhammed, it's your mind,
it's your soul or it's your sign, it's the Universe,
it's music, Mother Earth or Father Time, but
whatever name you give it, it's all One Power,

can't you see?
Whatever name you give it, it's the very air we
breathe.

It's the power of the love in you and me.

One Power. One Power. One Power.

It's the moment of creation.
It's an everlasting peace.
It's the freedom of forgiveness.
It's the sweetness of release.
It's the joy of inspiration.
It's the sunshine on your face.
It's the birthright of all nations.
It's the boundlessness of space.
It's the beauty of a baby,
The serenity of sleep.
It's the anger we abandon
For its love that's most deep.
It's One Power.
It's the power of the love that lives forever in you
and me.
It's the power of the love in you and me.
~Daniel Nahmod[3]

Prologue

Daniel's Gloves[4]

I sat, with two friends, in the picture window of a quaint restaurant just off the corner of the town-square. The food and the company were both especially good that day. As we talked, my attention was drawn outside, across the street. There, walking into town, was a man who appeared to be carrying all his worldly goods on his back. He was carrying, a well-worn sign that read, 'I will work for food.' My heart sank. I brought him to the attention of my friends and noticed that others around us had stopped eating to focus on him. Heads moved in a mixture of sadness and disbelief. We continued with our meal, but his image lingered in my mind. We finished our meal and went our separate ways. I had errands to do and quickly set out to accomplish them. I glanced toward the town square, looking somewhat halfheartedly for the strange visitor. I was fearful, knowing that seeing him again would call some response. I drove through town and saw nothing of him. I made some purchases at a store and got back in my car. Deep within me, the Spirit of God kept speaking to me: 'Don't go back to the office until you've at least driven once more around the square.' Then with some hesitancy, I headed back into town. As I turned the square's third corner, I saw him. He was standing on the steps of the church, going through his sack. I stopped and looked; feeling both compelled to speak to him, yet wanting to drive on. The empty parking space on the corner seemed to be a sign from God: an invitation to park. I pulled in, got out and approached the town's newest visitor. 'Looking for the pastor?' I asked. 'Not really,' he replied, 'just resting.' 'Have you eaten today?' 'Oh, I ate something early this morning.' 'Would you like to have lunch with me?' 'Do you have some work I could do for you?' 'No work,' I replied 'I commute here to work from the city, but I would like to take you to lunch.' 'Sure,' he replied with a smile. As he began to gather his things, I asked some surface questions. Where you headed?' 'St. Louis' 'Where you from?' 'Oh, all over; mostly Florida...' 'How long you been walking?' 'Fourteen years,' came the reply. I knew I had met someone unusual. We sat across from each other in the same restaurant I had left earlier. His face was weathered slightly beyond his 38 years. His eyes were dark yet clear, and he spoke with an eloquence and articulation that was startling He removed his jacket to reveal a bright red T-shirt that said, 'Jesus is The Never Ending Story.' Then Daniel's story began to unfold. He had seen rough times early in life. He'd made some wrong choices and reaped the consequences.. Fourteen years earlier, while

28

backpacking across the country, he had stopped on the beach in Daytona... He tried to hire on with some men who were putting up a large tent and some equipment. A concert, he thought. He was hired, but the tent would not house a concert but revival services, and in those services he saw life more clearly. He gave his life over to God. 'Nothing's been the same since,' he said, 'I felt the Lord telling me to keep walking, and so I did, some 14 years now.' 'Ever think of stopping?' I asked. 'Oh, once in a while, when it seems to get the best of me But God has given me this calling. I give out Bibles. That's what's in my sack. I work to buy food and Bibles, and I give them out when His Spirit leads.' I sat amazed. My homeless friend was not homeless. He was on a mission and lived this way by choice. The question burned inside for a moment and then I asked: 'What's it like?' 'What?' 'To walk into a town carrying all your things on your back and to show your sign?' 'Oh, it was humiliating at first. People would stare and make comments. Once someone tossed a piece of half-eaten bread and made a gesture that certainly didn't make me feel welcome. But then it became humbling to realize that God was using me to touch lives and change people's concepts of other folks like me.' My concept was changing, too. We finished our dessert and gathered his things. Just outside the door, he paused. He turned to me and said, 'Come Ye blessed of my Father and inherit the kingdom I've prepared for you. For when I was hungry you gave me food, when I was thirsty you gave me drink, a stranger and you took me in.' I felt as if we were on holy ground. 'Could you use another Bible?' I asked. He said he preferred a certain translation. It traveled well and was not too heavy. It was also his personal favorite... 'I've read through it 14 times,' he said. 'I'm not sure we've got one of those, but let's stop by our church and see.' I was able to find my new friend a Bible that would do well, and he seemed very grateful. 'Where are you headed from here?' I asked. 'Well, I found this little map on the back of this amusement park coupon.' 'Are you hoping to hire on there for a while?' 'No, I just figure I should go there. I figure someone under that star right there needs a Bible, so that's where I'm going next.' He smiled, and the warmth of his spirit radiated the sincerity of his mission. I drove him back to the town-square where we'd met two hours earlier, and as we drove, it started raining. We parked and unloaded his things. 'Would you sign my autograph book?' he asked... 'I like to keep messages from folks I meet.' I wrote in his little book that his commitment to his calling had touched my life. I encouraged him to stay strong. And I left him with a verse of scripture from Jeremiah, 'I know the plans I have for you, declared the Lord, 'plans to prosper you and not to harm you; Plans to give you a future and a hope.' 'Thanks, man,' he said. 'I know we just met and we're really just strangers, but I love you.' 'I know,' I said, 'I love you, too.' 'The Lord is good!' 'Yes, He is. How long has it been since someone hugged you?' I asked. A long time,' he replied. And so on the busy street corner in the drizzling rain, my new friend and I embraced, and I felt deep inside that I had been changed.. He put his things on his back, smiled his winning smile and said, 'See you in the New Jerusalem.'

(cont. in Epilogue)

Chapter 1: You are Connected to God— No Matter What

There must be an awareness that the presence of God is in everything.

When you believe you are separate from God, Universe, Spirit this belief is one of the world's greatest demises. People detach from God because they believe they are not good enough to be connected or loved by this all-knowing, all divine presence. When you believe this, you struggle to live a spiritually reliable life.

Various religions and denominations use moral codes to control their followers. They may prescribe certain codes constraining behavior and dress, for example. Some Protestant denominations forbid dancing and card-play, while others require their members to cover their heads. Believing your choices and paths are judged as right or wrong by those who follow a certain dogma may cause you to judge yourself. This leaves you feeling guilty and shamed, which ultimately leads you to believe you are not worthy of a connection to your Divine source. Everyone has done things in their lives, which they are not proud of and then, of course there is the phrase, *everyone is a sinner,* which has been coined by the Judeo-Christian concept. As I stated in the preface of this book:

Most of us were never introduced to God as an all-loving presence who supports us. Most of us were born and raised in family systems that believed God is judgmental and punishes us when we are bad. Many of us disconnect from this fierce God who will send us to hell if we do not follow the rules.

The idea that you are bad or wrong for experimenting with life is insane. Yes, you may have done things that you would prefer not to have flashed all over the TV screen during a super bowl commercial, but aren't those "experiments" part of life's journey? Are we not given the freedom to explore what we like and don't like in this life?

The most powerful and spiritually enlightened people on this earth have done some of the most random, spontaneous, undisciplined things in life. Those experiences were sometimes their greatest and wisest teachers, and without them, they would have never learned their lessons and transcended them into awareness of right choice. The walk of righteousness is the walk of grace. The definition of righteous is: right use.

Our biggest messes can become our message in life; they are the caution sign that slows us down, and helps us back to the right path. Without the mess and all the hard work of getting out of it, we might not make it to the next level.

Many spiritual leaders have been to the depths of hell to find themselves. Not that they choose consciously to walk into hell, but sometime in their life they found themselves lying with the dogs. Lying with the dogs will produce a great teacher because we teach what we need to learn the most.

Debbie Ford, the author of many best-selling spiritual books, shares openly about her addiction in her earlier years of life. She was in and out of rehab many times to clean up and only to walk out and start using again. She is a perfect example of someone who lay down with the dogs – meaning she went to the dark side of life. In the end, however, her darkness taught her what she did not want and was what dug out her life's purpose.

You alone are responsible for transforming your life, and transformation is not always the most beautiful thing to experience. God is not interested in what you experienced. Your spiritual enlightenment is what interests God. And, if you had to go down the wrong path to become enlightened, then was it really the wrong path?

You are enough just as you are. No thing, no title, no material possession, no bad or wrong experience matters in terms of defining who you really are. The ability to know this and to have this awareness of yourself is how you connect with God, the Divine within you, within all of us.

You are not your past; you are not all the things that happened to you. Your past does not define you. Who you were then, isn't who you are now. Who you are now, isn't who you will be. You are the infinite possibility of what can be. You are powerful and divine, and, as such, anything that interferes with your experience and expression of your authentic divine self must be addressed. The pure essence of who you are has nothing to do with what you did then. Instead of stressing over your past mistakes, learn, grow, and move on. Although the decisions you made yesterday may have played an important role in who you are today, remember that it is the decisions you make today that create the person you become tomorrow. Your divine essence is right there underneath your skin waiting to pour out of you in the perfect Divine moment. The Divine uses all of you and all the experiences you have to bring you to the perfect moment of divinity.

Divinity is the state of things that come from a supernatural power or deity, such as God, or spirit beings, and are therefore regarded as "divine" due to their unexplained nature. God is unexplainable because God is too big to comprehend the powerful forces that our universal laws are built on, and transcends human capacities. The word God is not big enough to describe the awesomeness of this all-encompassing, all loving divine presence that is in constant connection with you. However, it is not your job to figure it out. It is your job to live in the awareness that you are always in a constant divine relationship with God, and that you have special access to this magic just because you exist.

Your decisions do not exclude you from having a Divine relationship with God, because there is no place that the Divine begins or ends. The Divine is an all loving, all-powerful deity, which is beyond any words.

There must be an awareness that the presence of God is in everything.

The Divine is not limited to you; the Divine is of all consciousness throughout all eternity, throughout higher multi-universes, being one with that Divine all-powerful, all loving creator. Divine loving presence is everywhere in everything. There is no beginning or end; it is infinite space, infinite dimensions and all entireties. When you can completely understand this truth you will know then that all is well in all things.

Yes, unfortunately, bad things do happen like war that is fought in order to conquer people or exploit their resources, child abuse and the destruction of the earth. These acts may simply be blamed on humans who are not behaving in righteous ways, and have turned their back on the divine.

God knows the path to righteousness is not paved with purists. The bible clearly states that human beings cannot achieve righteousness through their own efforts. In order to choose the right ways we must experience life in its truest form. Not everyone will see the "right" way as his or her way. All wrong thinking had to be wiped away with righteous rags, and no one who walks, or who has walked this earth before left sparkling clean rags in their path.

All we can do is walk with faith and belief that where our journeys are leading us is exactly where we need to be to find our highest, truest selves. Without our experiences and life journeys we would not find our true connection to the Divine. It is all in divine order and divine timing. Getting over a painful experience is a lot like crossing monkey bars; to move forward, you have to let go at some point. God, will not leave you hanging out there because of something you did in your past.

You are to atone to your wrongdoings and enhance the results next time. When you know better, you do better. God desires to have a present, conscious relationship with you and knows you will show up mentally, emotionally, spiritually and physically when it's time, and that time is never too late. The key words here are *conscious relationships,* meaning you have a conscious understanding that you are connected to the Divine always, without interruption. There's no place God is not and this is the absolute law and truth of everything.

Does the fish know it was born in the water, or does it believe it is separate from the environment in which it lives? The fish probably doesn't have an understanding that it is in the water; it is simply a part of its survival to exist. If the fish were to leave the water the fish would die, but just because the fish died does not mean it is no more a part of this experience. We are like the fish that were born in the ocean and we all know that all oceans are connected as one. We cannot be separate from any ocean. Therefore, we humans are part of all things and all experiences, bad or good.

Even if you do not believe that it is true that the Divine is moving through you and all around you without interruption, it is. If anything, we all need to know we can lie down at the foot of the cross and start over today. Lying down at the foot of the cross is just a metaphor for life to begin anew; it is like hitting reset on a computer. If we feel we have been "thrown-out" of Heaven, so to speak, we sure do not want to go to God when it is time for that Divine appointment. We have all done things in our lives, with which we are not proud. But, you can redesign your life at any moment because each day is a new day for re-births. This moment is your choice and cannot be dictated by another person or the Divine. You may believe you are disconnected from God, but this is only a thought. As quickly as you feel you are not connected, you can change that thought and remember the truth that you are connected to the Divine no matter what, in an instant.

If there is sin, the *Course in Miracles* says sin could be defined as, "The perception we are separated from self and/or we are separated from our Creator." The truth is we are always connected and always being supported all the time by our Higher Power—no matter what. Each person has their own timeline and will experience their "Awe Ha's" in perfect timing. God is perfectly on time and never late.

I am being spiritually reliable; I am reminding you of this truth about you. You have a connection to God—no matter what. Connection to the Divine, Higher Power and your Source is unlimited and not just saved for the people who are doing perfectly well in the world. It means you can have a connection to God *always,* no matter what is happening or has happened in your life.

What a relief to remember you are loved by an all-powerful Divine presence that lives in you and all around you without interruption. It is perfect, you are perfect, all is in Divine timing; it is done in all things, right here and now, everywhere. Feel connected because it is already done in you and all around you. It just is.

Grounding Prayer

Dear God,
I pray for the absolute knowing within me that
the Divine is an all loving, all-encompassing
being of love. I know I am always connected to
God; the Divine without interruption and it is
impossible for me to be disconnected from my
source. I know when I feel disconnected from
you that this is only a lie I have told myself. I ask
for you to quickly let me remember the truth. I
know my decisions do not exclude me from
having a Divine relationship with you;
because there is no place you are not; nor any
place that the Divine begins or ends. I know the
Divine is an all-loving, all-powerful presence,
which is beyond any words. I know the Divine is
moving through me and is in everything. I know
you are an all-loving presence, infinitely
powerful creator of all things. You are in me,
everything, and in everyone always. Therefore,
all is well. And, so it is.

Chapter 2: God is an Elephant?[5]

Adapted from Lillian Quiqley

How one sees God is irrelevant
- Richard Seaman

There is a popular analogy used to show that all religions are valid ways to describe God. Religion professors especially love this philosophic analogy, because it equalizes all religions, making all religions equally "true" in their description of God.

The analogy is this: there are four blind men who discover an elephant. Since the men have never encountered an elephant, they grope about, seeking to understand and describe this new phenomenon. One grasps the trunk and concludes it is a snake. Another explores one of the elephant's legs and describes it as a tree. A third finds the elephant's tail and announces that it is a rope. And the fourth blind man, after discovering the elephant's side, concludes that it is, after all, a wall.

Each in his blindness is describing the same thing: an elephant. Yet each describes the same thing in a radically different way.

According to many, this is analogous to the different religions of the world—they are describing the same thing in radically different ways. Thus one should conclude that no individual religion has a corner on truth, but that all should be viewed as essentially equally valid.

This is a powerful and provocative image, and it certainly seems to capture something of the truth.

If God is infinite and we are finite, it is reasonable to believe that none of us can fully capture His nature. But does this philosophic analogy demonstrate the truth that all religions lead to God? To conclude that it does would ignore several points.

First, there is a fact of the matter: the elephant. What the blind men are attempting to describe is in fact an elephant, not something else. Just so, there are factual questions regarding God. "Does God even exist?" is a question of fact, much like, "Was Abraham Lincoln ever President of the United States?" If so, it would be true whether anyone believes it or not, and to deny it, one would be mistaken. Thus, not all opinions, whether concerning elephants or the nature of God, are equally true.

Second, all four blind men are, in fact, mistaken. It is an elephant and not a wall or a rope or a tree or a snake. Their opinions are not equally true—they are equally, and actually false. At best, such an analogy of religious pluralism would show that all religions are false, not true.

Third, and most important, the philosophic analogy does not take into account any kind of special revelation. If a fifth man was to arrive on the scene, one that could see (and who was able to demonstrate his credentials of having sight), and he were to describe the elephant as an elephant, and then it would change the analogy entirely.

Grounding Prayer:

It doesn't really matter what religion anybody believes. If their life is working (and there are many different approaches to life that are working very well) then why not let them believe whatever they want to believe? It's all working in the way that it is supposed to be. There are religions that you wouldn't want anything to do with, that are perfect mechanisms for the people who are involved in them. And therefore, they are a very good thing.

~ Abraham[6]

Chapter 3: My Path to God

The definition of spirituality is living an openhearted life – Oprah Winfrey[7]

One day while I was at work, waiting tables in my youth, my boss, Leslie walked up to me in the middle of my shift and handed me a book and said, "You need to read this".

Leslie was gifted, available and *spiritually reliable*. I did not recognize her attributes at the time. As I look back now I realize she possessed a knowing deep inside as she planted seeds of light into the world. She was a change agent and helped each and every person who she hired to connect to a greater sense of purpose within themselves, to see their gifts, not their shortcomings. Each experience was an opportunity for growth.

The title of the book was, *A Return to Love: Reflections on the Principles of "A Course in Miracles,"* by Marianne Williamson. I stared at her with a look of bewilderment on my face. I remember the word miracle grabbing me and holding my attention.

I asked her "Why should I read this book?"

"Because" she said, "I can tell you need to read it." I read it and it changed my life. Just read it." She walked away. I looked at the book and immediately threw it under the computer podium and forgot about it.

A few weeks went by and I went to work not having such great days. I was feeling down about my life but I cannot remember what the situation was. All of a sudden the word "miracle" popped into my head. "Yes, I sure could use a miracle in my life today" I spoke out in my thought. Then I remembered why I was thinking about miracles. Could that book still be under the podium? When I looked I could not see it, but as I reached further I found it buried underneath other things that had been thrown in there over the weeks. I grabbed it and immediately put it into my backpack knowing this time I really needed to read it.

The book stayed in my backpack, forgotten for a few more weeks. The only difference now was that everyday I would open my backpack and see the book looking at me as if to say, "Hello, I am here, open me when you are ready." I often have an immediate hesitation with books before I begin the journey of reading them because I know intuitively something is going to shift within me. I think it is the Scorpio within me that anchors in the resistance of evolving out of whatever situation I am experiencing in the given moment. I always seem to resist in the beginning when something good is about to shift in my life. I spent the next few months carrying the book around in the backpack. It became beaten and worn at the bottom of the bag. Every once in a while Leslie would ask me if I had started reading the book yet. I always had the same answer for her, "Not yet, but I am going to start reading it soon."

The Universe/God finally had enough of me procrastinating reading the book. All of the sudden I became very ill with a three-day flu. As I was laying the couch, bored and doing nothing when something nudged me and said, "It's time". I opened my backpack and dug deep into the bag. I pulled out the book. The cover was torn and the pages were frayed. I knew it did not change the content of the book. When I opened it to the first page something magical began to happen. I was drawn in like someone who was starving and reading a menu with all my favorite dishes on it. I felt like someone or something else had taken over and had began lifting me up into the freedom of reading without any effort. I kept saying aloud, "Wow" over and over again. It was the first time in my search for religious and spiritual truth that things made sense to me. I could not stop reading it. I felt like a dry sponge in the desert, which had just received the monsoon rains. I was absorbing it as quickly as I could read it and could not get enough. In my knowing I felt I already knew this information and I was being reminded of it. How could I have known this? I just knew that I knew I had found that for which I had been searching.

I realized I had been searching for my connection to God in a box, a restricted space with limited content inside of it. This book filled me up and gave me what I call "truth bumps." It did not leave me questioning God, religion, church, worship, Holy Sprit, right, wrong, good and evil and my role in the drama called life. Nothing had made sense to me like this did. I knew without a shadow of a doubt that I had finally found my truth! And, what was so exciting and mind blowing was I did not find my truth inside the four walls of a church. I found my truth inside a book called, A *Return to Love*[8] which had no agenda or any claim on any one religious belief.

I had finally opened a door that made sense to my soul. The only way I can describe it is: I had found peace, love and acceptance within this vast, open space. I had found a place, which was tolerant and encouraged me to walk my own path openheartedly the way I felt was right for me. All I knew was I had to move towards this thing called Spirituality.

The next few years were very interesting because I became a self-help junkie. Spending hours in the aisles of bookstores touching and reading everything I could get my hands on that were even remotely related to Spirituality, self-help or personal empowerment. Not every book had the same effect on me that *Return to Love* did but what I know is they all had pieces of truth within their pages. I did not always resonate with every writer or concept, but again I knew without saying it that this may be someone else's book of truth.

I am holding a piece of the Universe in my hands and in my heart. I want to share it with anyone who will listen. I am euphoric and grounded in the concept of "less is more." In the beginning I had to develop a fine discernment when I choose to share my spiritual truths as they related to my experience. The word "overwhelming" comes to mind because I was so passionate about my enlightenments I wanted to shout it out in every venue or gathering of which I was a part. I soon learned not everyone wanted to hear my epiphanies or realizations.

　　　If you are reading this book you may be relating to this story. Throughout my years of coaching, teaching and sharing with others I have heard this story over and over, always with unique twists and turns as it relates to an individual's soul journey. We all want to feel like we are connected to something bigger than we are. We all want to be understood, seen, valued and validated by others and more importantly to confirm that our life has a specific journey and purpose. A few of the most important questions we, as human souls, search to have answered are the following:

1)　　What is my life purpose?

2)　　What happens when I die and where do I go?

3)　　Is there another dimension of time and space, which exists in conjunction to this reality?

4) Is the existence of heaven and hell real?
5) Does a God/Higher Power exist and what form does it take?

6) What does this all mean to be in the life that I am living? Why I am here?

You may find the answers to these questions in this book, but I do not know the answers, as they would relate to you. The truth is, you must search deep within yourself to find these answers for yourself. You do this while customizing your personal relationship with that energy you define has your Higher Power.

What I find interesting is if we went out into the hub of a busy city and asked people on the streets these questions you would get just as many different and diverse answers as there are people to ask. The answers are as individual and unique as we all are in this life experience. However, there may be some common threads of truth. You will not find these answers inside a church, a confessional or a temple; but then again these vessels may provide an insight or pathway enabling you to expand your spiritual truth as it relates to you. You may find the answers to these questions inside the Bible, a book, a conversation, a movie, a connection with another person, a class you take, a life experience or maybe just simply within yourself.

I am diligently committed to being a messenger of clarity and remaining open to all truth and all possibility. I know there are many pathways and journeys that guide us to God. You can call it God; you can call it Universe or you can call it Spirit. Sometimes I refer to *IT* as G.U.S. (God, Universe, Spirit) but it doesn't matter what you call it because they all lead to the same Source. There is only One Power and this is a Divine Power that moves through you and around you without interruption. Even if you do not believe in this Divine Power, it still is happening, working and co-creating for every soul who lives or does not live – it just is!

My gift is to share with you pivotal lessons in life, lessons of *spiritual reliability*. These teachings have taken me deep within my knowing, driven by a higher presence, guiding me deep within my own spiritual intuition, my truth. Intuition is a spiritual faculty and does not explain, but simply points the way.

Thank you Leslie for showing me you can find a piece of truth even in a little restaurant job.

I am including a grounding prayer from the teachings of Ernest Holmes who is the founder of Science of Mind. This is one of my many own truths. May you find your own truth within yourself and through the countless vessels that exist in the universe, which are moving through and around you at all times, always supporting your existence.

Grounding Prayer

I know there is a Power for Good, which is responding to me and bringing into my experience everything that is necessary for my unfoldment, to my happiness, to my peace, to my health, and to my success. I know there is a Power for Good that enables me to help others and to bless the whole world. So I say quietly to myself: There is one Life, that Life is God, that Life is perfect, that Life is my life now. It is flowing through me, circulating in me. I am one with Its rhythm. My heart beats with the pulsation of the Universe, in serenity, in peace, and in joy. My whole, physical being is animated by the Divine Spirit, and if there is anything in it that does not belong, it is cast out because there is One Perfect Life in me now. And I say to myself: I am guided daily so that I shall know what to do under every circumstance, in every situation. Divine Intelligence guides me in love, in joy, and in complete self-expression. Desiring that the Law of Good alone shall control me, I bless and prosper everything I am doing. I multiply every activity. I accept and expect happiness and complete success. Realizing that I am one with all people, I affirm that there is a silent Power flowing through them, and me, which blesses and heals and prospers, makes happy and glad their pathway.
And realizing that the world is made up of people like myself, I bless the world and affirm that it shall come under the Divine government

of Good, under the Divine providence of Love, and under the Divine leadership of the Supreme Intelligence. For thine is the kingdom, and the power, and the glory, for ever.

Amen and So, it is[9]

Chapter 4: What is Spiritual Reliability?

Spiritual reliability is being loyal and obedient to the truth of spirit as it arrives in each moment.

The definition of Spiritual Reliability is:

The act of **doing** what it is you are hearing, feeling, seeing and knowing. It is acting with your body through doing, speaking and showing up for a greater higher purpose. It is knowing you are being utilized to do the work here and now. It is the act of serving and asking the question, "How may I serve?" and then acting with your life as a vessel to be utilized for a greater higher purpose. It is knowing that you are the hands, voice, ears and feet with which the Universe does its work.

It is knowing that for you to be free with who you are, you must connect and align yourself with Spirit. You have faith in a Divine presence and you know this presence will take you where you need to be. Spiritual Reliability is about being willing to go on, even when you cannot see the path beneath your feet. Perhaps you cannot see what is beyond the bend either, but you trust in the flow of life. You are obedient to the Divine and you are willing to spiritually listen as you are nudged then act with your life for a greater higher purpose.

The Eight Guiding Principles to Living a Spiritually Reliable Life:

1) I am committed to Divine higher guidance and I understand that I co-create my life with the Divine.

2) I am willing to be utilized for a greater higher purpose.

3) I operate from a high level intention to serve.

4) My contribution to the world is an up level and I ask myself: How can I serve, rather than what can I get?

5) I take time to breathe, get calm and quiet my mind in order to hear God's whispers.

6) I hear, feel, see and sense Divine guidance as it arrives.

7) I show up where God needs me next, and in doing so, this allows my life to be utilized for a greater higher purpose.

8) I know that I am always connected to the Divine without interruption and there is no place God is not.

Most people in the world believe the only thing required is to show up physically in body and form. There is a lack of presentness in the world at a far greater degree than ever before. We must learn how to show up in much more powerful ways than just being physically present. When you do show up in physical form, are you totally in the moment? Are you completely in the conversation? Are you present and listening from your deepest level? Many of us lack the awareness of how to be present. We believe that showing up simply in our body is being present. However, have you ever been in a room with a bunch of people, only to find yourself feeling empty, unseen, not connected and ignored?

When you show up in life disconnected, not being present, it is less likely that you will be utilized for the greater higher good. This is because you are not fully present to the higher, spiritual possibilities that surround you that may potentially need your attention. A spiritually reliable person understands that in order for his or her life to be utilized for a greater higher purpose, they must become fully present to how they are showing up in the world, and decide to show up on all levels—physically, mentally, emotionally and spiritually.

The world wants to offer more ways of connecting with others, but the people have lost their ability to have face-to-face real time interactions with one another. Our world is going faster and faster—technology is increasing the ability to not have to rely on human connections because now we can text message, email, and social media our way through life. People are more present to their mobile devices than they are to other human beings. You can walk around in an airport, mall, school, or work and watch, as people are being totally present to their mobile machines. You can see people everywhere staring into a phone attached to their hands, walking like zombies and staring into a 3x2 screen. What are they all doing? Are they searching for meaning, for information, or for connections?

I have watched people sit down to share a meal with another person whom they call a "friend" and the instant a text message or email pops up the in-person connection is instantly lost, with all the attention going to the mobile device. It's as if they will miss out on something very important if they do not stop and give all their attention to the machine that just notified them of a spam email or a friend texting, "What's up"?

As a writer I like to make sure my intuitional claims are correct and try to find other sources that support my claims. I ran across a very supportive article written by Ben Mester from Article-Dashboard.com. He describes what I am referring to perfectly.

"As 12.21.12 has come and gone, one of the beliefs has been that the world has shifted into a higher level of consciousness. Yes, the Mayan calendar ended on 12.21.12 and many prophecies shared that these are the ends of the days of the world. Is it possible that these shifts are the shifts into presentness? Are we entering into a new age of presentness? The shift from yang to yin? Meaning the shift from masculine energies to feminine energies?

In the Taoist philosophy, *yin* is the feminine principle, representing the forces of the earth, while *yang* is the masculine principle, representing spirit. When God is referred to as *He*, then all humanity becomes *She*. This isn't a man-woman issue. Reference to God as a masculine principle in no way impinges on feminist conviction. Our feminine self is just as important as our masculine.

"The right relationship between male and female principle is one in which the feminine surrenders to the masculine. Surrender is not weakness or loss. It is a powerful nonresistance. Through openness and receptivity on the part of human consciousness, spirit is allowed to infuse our lives, to give meaning and direction. Mary symbolizes the feminine within us, which is impregnated by God. The *Yin* female energies that allow this process and are fulfilled by surrendering into it. This is not weakness on her part; it is strength. The Christ on earth is fathered by God, and mothered by our humanness. Through a mystical connection between the human and divine, we give birth to our higher self". –Course in Miracles[10]

"Was 12.21.12 a message of balance? Did the world recalibrate itself? What will happen to all the yin resistant energies? Could it be that we as a human civilization have lost our ways, forgotten how to connect, be present and have real time connections?

It's ironic to me that we call the modern era the age of communication. A lack of communication is listed as the leading cause of breakdowns in marriages and relationships. Our current era has a higher divorce rate than we have ever seen before. I came across an interesting bible quote awhile back that explains this phenomenon very well. "The more the words, the less the meaning, and how does that profit anyone?"[11]

That quote is more than 3000 years old, but it sums up our current age of communication perfectly and points us directly into a deeper era of communication; sometimes less is more.

It struck me because it reminded me much of our modern era. In our modern era, communication abounds with text messaging, emails, and constant updates on Facebook and twitter. But, meaningful communication seems to be dwindling rapidly. It's becoming easier to have deeper level text messaging conversations than a real time and live conversation. Is it possible to say that the reasoning is because when you give a man a mask he will tell you all his secrets?

The age of communication is almost like a great roar drowning out the honest, rare whispers of wise counsel that often are lost in the fray of everything else going on. Our age of communication seems like a sham — an age that knows less words, yet preaches them all the louder in order to make up for it. An age that has nothing new to contribute, but speaks the same dribble all the louder just to make up for the lack of present, real, honest, transformational communication, which all people are seeking.

The age of communication seems similar to yet another modern phenomenon: ambient light. There is a hilltop by my home that I often visit at night to watch the distant city just beyond it. There it sits, enshrouded in a glow of low-level brightness pervading the night world. Though the ambient light is good for those traveling through the city, those wishing to gaze upward at the stars beyond are hindered and unable to take in the array of tiny lights.

Our age of communication seems the same. Though we as humans communicate more now than ever before, we have not learned how to communicate meaningfully, and our words are drowned in a hum of mediocrity. And because of our constant communications with those around us, we never perceive what a treasure real communication is, living a life blind to the vast array of twinkling thoughts that lie just overhead.

Both the Hopis and Mayans recognize that we would approach the end of a World Age. In both cases, however, the Hopi and Mayan elders did not prophesize that everything will end.

Rather, this is a time of transition from one world age into another. The message they gave concerns our making a choice of how we enter the future ahead. You can choose to move through this shift with either resistance or acceptance, but the choice you make will determine whether the transition happens with devastating changes or gradual peace and tranquility. The same theme can be found reflected in the prophecies of many other Native American visionaries. The key is moderation.

The world has become unbalanced and is tilting too far to one side. It is time to make a significant shift in the way we show up in our relationships, bringing awareness, purpose and importance to being present and balanced in our daily lives. We have forgotten the importance of real, significant, "present" human exchange."

Many people in the world have stopped having relationships because they think that there are too many distractions to juggle. Our new normalcy in relationships has become a jungle ride of surprises that come from every direction. Most of us do not feel heard, seen, or think that what we are saying to one another matters. You feel this way because you are competing with the age of communication.

Oprah Winfrey says there are four basic needs in every person's life. These four needs are:

1. Do you see me?
2. Do you hear me?

3. Do you believe me?
4. Does what I am saying to you matter?

ALL life matters and the fact that you made it to where you are now, makes you worthy. You matter — all life matters. Today, most people feel life is empty and meaningless. The humans of this world are calling out to be seen and heard at a greater level than ever before. Most of us are in such psychological pain, thus are spinning, grabbing and tugging to make meaning of this life. We have lost our ways, lost the backbone and foundation and most importantly the purpose of being here on earth. The purpose is to have present relationships and know that the "relationship is the classroom for the Holy Spirit." Without relationships we do not grow and evolve. The Mayan's were forecasting an era of humanity in which humans became very unbalanced in their presentness to one another. Modern people have become more present to technology in this life, and have forgotten that we are human beings being left behind and our internal souls are withering away.

The newer generations are growing up with social media as their way of connecting with others. This is not normal and I do not believe we can survive fully in our natural humanness with this as our normal. When was the last time you sat around a dinner table, totally unplugged and totally present with those at the table?

In the next chapter I will teach you, The

Four States of Presentness. My intention is to put a dent into your soul, bring awareness of choice so you can snap out of it, unplug and come back to wholeness, balance, moderation and learn to be present with those whom you love, those whom you encounter and those whom are among the living.

Grounding Prayer

Dear God,
I say Yes to staying fully present to my life and those who are a part of my experience. I live in balance and moderation, between the two worlds—Human being and Technology. I can become a part of each without losing myself in either world. I dance between both with grace and harmony and enjoy my experiences. I release this into the Law of God as done. And, so it is.

Chapter 5: The Four States of Presentness

The greatest recent demise to our world has been the lack of real communication.

One of the biggest obstacles to living a spiritually reliable life is to not be fully present. The universe needs a willing player in its plan. Living a spiritually reliable life must come with the awareness that we are spirit's tool. We must walk each day, each moment carrying this awareness into every experience we have. To walk a spiritually reliable life will require commitment and absolute faith that you are always connected to the divine in every moment. When we walk carrying these knowns, we then become willing to be utilized for a greater higher purpose, which is to be Spirit's tool.

The first thing we must do in order for spirits energy to co-create with ours is we must plug into source. Source is like an electrical outlet in your house. It's always there, and always on. It is your job to plug into its energy and allow that energy to fuel you. You are God's instrument and you must learn how to plug into the all flowing, all knowing source of divine energies of which everyone is a part. This energy is non-partial, not threatening to you and will flow through you and everyone without judgment. This energy is willingly available for you to use it, and the quickest way to plug into it is to become present. We must become fully present on all four levels. In this chapter I will be addressing the four states of being present.

What is Presentness?

Meaning: The quality of being the Present. A moment or period in time between past and future – totally in the now. At the present time; right now. Immediate, not in the past or future.

Context example:

- the time when something happens.
- the property of belonging to the present time.[12]

Present State #1: Physically Present

Physically Present is showing up physically in real-time, in the here and now. Taking your body to a physical location where people come together to be together.

    To physically arrive is the first step to being present. However, it requires much more than just arriving. We have all been in situations and moved through the obstacles of getting somewhere, and when we arrive it wasn't what we were expecting because something seemed to be missing or felt "off" when we got there.
    What might be missing is your ability to feel safe and secure in this moment, and you

must slowly acclimate yourself into the space. Everyone has a sixth sense and sometimes our gut knowing needs time to discern our safety when we arrive into a new space and place. When you arrive into new environments or even places you have been before, it takes time to acquaint and reacquaint yourself with the new energies, new people, and it is smart to ground yourself when you arrive each time.

I invite you to ground yourself by slowing down once you get there. Take in the scenery and the energies that are moving through the space. Become aware of yourself and stand in noticing yourself as you take in the newness. Assessing the environment is needed in order for anyone to feel safe.

You may want to find a seat once you arrive and just let yourself absorb everything and take it all in. Find a quiet space where you can be alone for a few minutes and remind yourself to come into the space, take a few deep breaths and see yourself as whole and complete. When you feel yourself calm down, surround yourself in loving blue light. Blue light ushers in perfect balance between physical and spiritual worlds, and gives you inner peace, deep feelings, high level communication and great faith. Once you begin to feel safe and secure then you can begin to mingle and socialize. To physically arrive is another way we can live a spiritual reliable life.

Grounding Mantra to physically arrive:

I, _____ say yes to physically arriving now in this space and place. I surround myself in loving blue light protecting me from all negativity, unbalance, fear or lack. I breathe in this beautiful, peaceful, healing, faithful, blue light into every organ, cell and nerve within my body. I see this healing blue light protecting and encircling me. I feel safe, secure and ready to be here now. I walk forward grounded and anchored to my faith that I am connected to the divine in all things.
And, so it is.

Present State #2: Mentally Present

Mentally Present is preparing yourself mentally by shutting down all conversations within your own mind that do not pertain to this moment.

To mentally arrive is the second step to being present and another way to live a spiritually reliable life. Most of us arrive with many mental thoughts rushing through our minds. If you are thinking about your day at work, the phone conversation you were having, your grocery list, your bills that need to be paid, your travel plans or anything else, you are not mentally present. Many of us have a very hard time shutting down our heads (those constant backward or forward thoughts) and the mental racket of distractions. Our minds are like pinball machines and our thoughts are firing, pinging off the walls of our cranial cortexes. When you think about a past situation or a future situation to come–you are actually hallucinating. The only thing that is real is now and everything else is an illusion.

Becoming mentally present is like training a new puppy. Our minds can be very immature and need to be taught the correct way. Our immature minds are very selfish and like to be distracted with a lot of stimuli. We thrive off of drama in an addictive way, and our world is rushing now at a greater pace than ever before. We are plugged into our technology and we are available 24 hours a day. The Mind – the wandering mind is programmed to multi-task in many different arenas and can have a very hard time shutting down its programming.

The three things a puppy needs in order to be trained properly are: Consistency, Discipline and Follow- through. When a puppy is beginning its potty training we have to show it where it is supposed to go to the bathroom. We have to show it the boundaries – the in and out of bounds. Most puppies have a very short attention span, somewhat like our human minds. However, with consistency, discipline and follow-through, eventually the puppy understands what it needs to do and will learn to focus its mind on the right behaviors and feelings.

Our minds are very similar to a puppy's mind because we lack focus and are more interested in the things that distract us. With consistency, discipline and follow-through we will begin to train our minds to stay mentally present -meaning, when the puppy lifts its leg in the house we need to be very present to the puppy doing this and crack down immediately with a negative reinforcement and always following through with consistent discipline and behavior.

We can apply this to training our mind by noticing when we are mentally distracted and lack focus. When you notice you have drifted off into another thought and missed half of something someone just shared with you, you did exactly the same thing the puppy does when it drifts outside the potty area. You will need to call your mind back to the present, and reset yourself each time you notice you are drifting away. The more you catch yourself and the quicker you catch yourself, the faster you will learn to stay present. Eventually, working that part of your mind's muscle, it will become a new normal and you will find yourself living a mentally present life.

Grounding mantra to become mentally present:
I _____ arrive now into this place and space easily and allow my mind to let go of anything that does not pertain to this moment. I trust and allow the universe to handle the details of my life, and I know there is a time for everything, and even this moment is full of possibility. I let it go and I know that whatever is going on in my life can be handled when I get there. I know there is nothing I can do right now, but to be here. I can deal with any situation

outside of this when I arrive in that moment. I am totally mentally present. And, so it is.

Present State #3 Emotionally Present

Emotionally present is stepping into a heart space of love, compassion, empathy, sympathy and devotion; activating and tapping into the heart center of the moment; calling up all loving thoughts within you and seeing through the eyes of love; responding, as opposed to reacting.

Every living person is experiencing their life through their own lenses. The reality of it is that they are in their own mind and are experiencing life as it is neurologically filtered through them. We all have experienced dramatic, stressful or overwhelming moments in our lives, and at that time the only thing in your mind was the "nerve racking" situation. Then you snap out of it and realize what you were doing and thinking. We have all gone insane for moments of time. This is life for all people and we must realize people will be people. One of the most profound quotes in my opinion is: **"The relationship is the classroom for the *Holy Spirit*" – C.I.M.**[13]

Without relationships you do not grow, evolve or stretch yourself to the next level. Relationships are the classrooms for essential growth and they will teach you various ways to manage your life. One requirement of being in relationships with others is having emotional compassion for them. Seeing through the eyes of love and doing your best to allow them to be where they are, and knowing everyone is having their own journey in life. In order for you to do this you must be able to lead with empathy, sympathy and compassion. When you allow these attributes to lead you, you live a very powerful life; a life of service to others, which contributes to the overall good for all involved.

When you are emotionally present you tune into a higher level of energy and view all experiences through the eyes of compassion. Living from an emotional state of being sees that all pain is the same – my pain or your pain. All humans can tap back into their pain from a past experience. When we do this, we call it empathy, and the feelings of empathy are what connects us all and helps us to remember we are all one big ball of connected energy, moving simultaneously, but in different directions.

Death feels like death, divorce feels like divorce, sickness feels like sickness, joy feels like joy, happiness feels like happiness and love feels like love. You cannot be detached from any of these attributes if you are emotionally present and have experienced these feelings before. All humans have experienced all and possibly more of these feelings, and everyone has the ability to show up emotionally present if they choose.

Some people do not want to feel emotion and many of us have been told not to show our emotions. Just because you show your vulnerability, does not mean you lose your creditability. When you are told emotions show weakness and lessen your creditability, this belief within itself destroys the emotional undercurrent of your soul.

When you were born, you were born as a perfect and loving being. You came into this world with a veil of mystical light and this veil kept out anything that was not of love. You did not know right or wrong, good or bad, black or white. If you have ever had children or simply been around children then you know that there is something very magical about this age. It is magical for both the observer and the infant. You were only programmed to love, to see through the lenses of love and to be an empathic person. However, as you got older you unlearned your original programming to love and were taught fear, lack, wrong, right, black, white, good, bad and judgment. Your state of wholeness was jaded and you began to see through the lenses of fear. As Marianne Williamson states in her book, *Return to Love*, "What we were born with is love, what we have learned here is fear."[14]

When we decide to show up emotionally present in every encounter we then begin to break down the walls that keep us separate from one another and then the miracles begin to take place.

If we show up reacting and are emotionally charged we then co-create with a negative and an uncompassionate mind. This is another way we can struggle to live a spiritually reliable life.

Grounding mantra to become emotionally present:

I _____ say yes to being emotionally present. I connect to my heart now and extend love into each situation. I co-create my life with the Divine mind and arrive emotionally now. I show up as a spiritually reliable vessel with a clean compassionate emotional state of mind. I am a life force filled with compassion, empathy, sympathy and devotion for all. I am emotionally present. And, so it is.

Present State #4 Spiritually Present

Spiritually Present is having a knowing you have a divine appointment with each and every person whom you have the opportunity to have an encounter with; being miracle ready and being ready to see the bigger, higher, greater spiritual lessons.

To spiritually arrive is the fourth step to being present and another way we live a spiritually reliable life. See every encounter and every situation as a divine appointment for all who are involved. When you arrive in a space or place, be willing to ask the question, "How may I use my life for the greater higher good of all?"

You are activating the spiritual law of attraction directly to you. When you ask such a powerful question you are actually plugging into God's mind, which gives you the ability to connect directly to a universal level of service.

This higher level is connected to a superior thought form, as opposed to believing you are a separate mind. You were made from this universal mind; therefore, your only task is to plug into it *willingly*. Human beings are programmed to love naturally, and love comes from G.U.S. - God, Universe and Spirit. However, for God to utilize your mind there must be a willingness to serve in a loving way. God will not take away your free will and you are totally free to roam in this human form as you wish. You can either use your life to serve the greater higher good or your can use your life in caustic ways.

To spiritually arrive is to make a very important high-level decision to use your life as an instrument of peace. When you make this very important commitment to step it up and to spiritually arrive you are given a very different pair of eyes to view the world through. These are the eyes of God and God see's every encounter as an opportunity to bring a piece of light, a piece of truth and to see that every encounter is a divine encounter. As an instrument of peace you see every soul as uniquely special and know that there are no random accidents and every person has a purpose.

An instrument of peace is someone who sets the intention to bring light to every encounter. Where there is hatred they bring love. Where there is doubt they bring faith. Where there is falsehood they bring truth. Where there is pain they bring comfort. Where there is silence they bring grace. Where there is despair they bring wholeness. Where there is blindness they bring sight. Where there is darkness they bring light. With every word they speak, they do not seek to be heard, but to hear and to console. It is not about being seen, but to see and to be the presence of love. For when you give love, you will receive love.

When you make the extraordinarily important choice to be an instrument of peace in the world, you bring peace to every person and every encounter you have. Even if you think you did not put a positive dent into someone's life, you did because you co-created your encounter with the divine. The divine is flawless and the divine uses all willing people to serve ITS purpose.

A spiritually reliable vessel knows, *when you forgive your fellow man they will find reprieve. A spiritually reliable person knows that they are connected to all life—no matter how insignificant it is perceived to be. You know that all you have and all you feel, is because of God's love that is pouring into you, from the ultimate divine source, which is connected to every nerve, fiber and cell within you. "You know that all you reap is all you sow. You know that all love coming to you or from you is living proof of this truth. You thank the divine for everything you* see, experience and be. You stand in grace and gratitude and thank the divine. You know that seasons come and go no matter what you choose. You know that there is a thousand miles of roads that all lead to one simple truth. This truth is Love." – *Olivia Newton-John, Grace and Gratitude*[15]

Grounding mantra to become spiritually present:

I _____ say yes to being spiritually present now. I do this by seeing every encounter as a divine appointment where I can bring a piece of peace to every soul with whom I connect. I co-create my life force with the divine mind and I am willing to serve the divine purpose. I walk forward as an instrument of peace now. I hear, see, console and am the presence of forgiving love. And, so it is.

Chapter 6: Forgiveness— Letting go of grudges and Bitterness

Forgiveness is the quickest way to release you from your inner and outer struggles, issues, conflicts and dis-eases.

Many of us believe that to forgive someone for a wrongdoing is to send him or her a message that what he or she did was ok. The opposite is true and the fact is when you forgive someone else for their acts you actually release yourself from the physical, mental, emotional, spiritual distress and disharmony it causes you. When you hold onto such low vibrational energy it stops you from expressing your true God/divine nature into the world and from that mental stance you will struggle to live a spiritually reliable life.

The act of forgiving others is the highest expression of Gods divine nature and is the only way you can truly become free and to move around the cabin of life in harmony, so to speak. When you make a decision to not forgive another for what they did or said to you, then you become firmly belted and restricted into a very limited space lacking possibilities. Think of how you feel when you are sitting in the middle seat in an airplane. Being belted and strapped down onto any chair only keeps you stuck and anchored to a very limited space. In this metaphor I'm describing a very small space with limited room to move, grow and express yourself fully. This small-constricted, confining space may feel safe and comfy, but lacks the open space for true bigger possibility to manifest.

All of us have had acts, words and wrong doings done to us. And, most of those acts of wrongdoing were perceived as painful by our human ego.

Is it possible that these acts of wrongdoing were powerful learning opportunities? Life is full of wrong doings, misfortune, drama and chaos. The light is not the only teacher. The darkness teaches and shows you what you don't want in your life. These experiences never feel peaceful, but come with a message if you let your spirit guide you. As Marianne Williamson writes, "The ego says, "Once everything falls into place, I'll feel peace." The spirit says, "Find your peace, and then everything will fall into place."[16]

When these types of experiences happen to us we take it very personally and our automatic emergency response system goes into high alert and rings the danger bell. These bells signal a rude intrusion, a breach in contract. They beckon and warn you of a threat and possible betrayal to your physical, mental, emotional and spiritual systems. When we hear the bells of betrayal sound out, most of us run, hide, duck and take cover seeking to avoid or minimize our own personal/spiritual attack – this is normal for most of us and is a part of our human programming. This programming is literally hardwired into us from our DNA and goes way back to our primitive self's. This programming is designed to protect us and sends the message to fight or flight – not to forgive those who have hurt our emotional selves.

The process of rewiring our primitive self is not something we naturally do easily. In fact, it will feel very unnatural and odd until you retrain and rewire your mental-chemical programming. In the beginning most people will resist the idea to forgive someone for an act of wrongdoing and will cling to their pain, agony and misery out of sheer fear of being violated again. I am a firm believer and teach that healing can only begin to take place after you feel the pain. I always tell my students, who are feeling an old wound during class to talk it out it, walk it out, run it out, dance it out, do something with the feelings, but make sure you feel them. In order to heal you must feel, and then once we feel, we must deal. Nothing has a hold on your mind that you cannot release. To break free you will need to go through a spiritual labor and seek to give birth to your higher self–a higher self is the part of you who can rise up and be forgiving. It's just a moment where you decide to let go of right and wrong, bear down to feel the pain you once experienced. Then begin to apply love to anything that is perceived as hurt, pain, betrayal and/or a lack of love–in this moment you will rise up, transcend the old stuck negative stories and feelings and move into compassion for the wrong doer.

It is like a 1000 pound weight is lifted off your chest and you can breath again. Most people do not realize how much pressure was on them until they let it go and forgive. To forgive is extremely relieving to our mind, body and *spirit*. To forgive is to love, and to lovingly forgive is to walk a *Spiritually Reliably* life.

A few years back I started working with a client who was new to coaching. Generally I refer to myself as a mind, body, wellness coach, but when I did it seemed to stir something up within him and it quickly became the topic of discussion. I was alert to his reaction to the title: *Mind, Body Wellness Coach*.

My awareness was that his ego seemed to be quickly activated by the mere mention of the title. Ego, *edging God out* would be appropriate in this case, because as I began to listen to him speak about his life, it became very obvious that his ego wanted nothing to do with wellness of his mind or body.

As I began to ask him questions about his life, I quickly picked up that he was holding on to a mountain of unforgiveness. He told me when he was 10 years old both his parents were killed by a drunk driver. His life became a nightmare in a blink of an eye. The story he shared only became weightier.

At 10 years old the only solidity he knew was ripped out from beneath him. He was put into foster care where his life became horrendous. A few weeks after he entered he began to get molested night by night by another young man in the residence. The nightly abuse began to take its toll and eventually resulted in the loss of his voice due to his fear. He began to accept the nightly exploitations because he felt he had no one to turn to and thought God was punishing him because he had horrifying thoughts of one day finding the man who killed his mother and father and assassinating him. He only knew one thing—Vengeance.

He lived everyday of his life holding on to the vengeful thoughts and none of these negative thoughts and beliefs were serving him to be the best version of himself. He ran away from every home he was put into, then in time started to live on the street. He found a way to deaden his pain through drugs. He began to get a hold of drugs by selling his body to any man or women who would pay for it. His fix was heroin, costing him $30.00, marking the worth of his body. He spent over two decades living this type of lifestyle, and as a consequence he became HIV+ at the age of 16 and lives with Hepatitis C. He spent over an hour sharing with me all he had experienced and witnessed.

I asked him whom he had told about his thoughts of wanting to kill the man who unintentionally killed his parents? He said, "No one, until now." At this moment I fully realized he had been holding on to anger, hatred, resentment, pain and victimness since he was 10 years old.

Any thoughts of revenge are like cancer eating you from the inside, which then manifests into your life as pain, sickness, addiction, isolation, shame, anger, fear and then turns inward and becomes an even deeper wound that creates a self-sacrificed life.

I asked him if he would be willing to just speak out everything that was on his mind. He agreed and the torrent began. As he shared it, it continued to get larger, bigger and longer. It was like the door to Pandora's box was opened and what exposed itself was unbelievable darkness, negativity and hatred. All of this was stealing and robbing him from having a beautiful life, a life where he walked daily as his greatest, highest, wisest expression of himself. Instead it was stealing and robbing his authentic personal power.

In this moment I felt like a tornado had just hit the room. He and I both became very silent and held very direct, loving eye contact. Then he spoke out, "Oh my God, I can't believe all of those things that were inside of me, and buried deep like a parasite clinging and robbing me from having the life I deserve. I have never talked to anyone about this. I have been living this way for so many years, and now by me just speaking out this stuff it feels like a 1000 pound weight has been lifted of my chest." At this moment I noticed there was a new expression on his face, which I had never seen previously. It was like a light bulb went off in his brain. I asked him, "What?"

He said, "I have to let go of the hatred for this man because not only did he kill my parents, but I am now allowing him to kill me and all my dreams. The hatred and lack of forgiveness I live with everyday has stolen so much of me. In order for me to move on and have a life beyond the one I currently know, I must forgive him and release the pain to God. I know my parents are ok."

"Yes," I said, "Yes!" I had an image in this moment that champagne bottles were popping off in heaven and his parents and God were celebrating his new awareness, a new life of forgiveness! I believe there will be copious amount of work to be done by this young man, but what I do know is he has begun a new life, a new way, he had a shift in perception, which began to create a new normal, a happier more fulfilling life, full of possibility, with forgiveness for his biggest nemesis and compassion for himself.

If you are still living in the pain of any experience, you may need to feel it for a while. I know that everyone is on his or her own timeline and God will always honor your time by allowing you to choose. Remember there is no wrong path and even the path of pain, can become, in the end, your greatest and wisest teacher. While journeying down this path of forgiveness I believe you will be in one of three metaphorical models and may vacillate between the mindsets:

1) **Ostrich:** The Ostrich archetype chooses to hang on to the pain of the experience for their own conscious or unconscious reasons. Burying their head in the sand, denying there is anything wrong. Walking in a fog, not able to see clearly or consciously.

2) **Masochist:** The Masochist archetype enjoys the pain—feeling alive because it appears that something is happening in their life. They may be enthralled by the drama, and choose to hang out in it because it's feeding a need within them to feel something, or rather–this is better than nothing.

3) **Warrior:** The Warrior archetype feels the *need* to feel the pain and to learn the lessons by getting squeezed and pushed through the knothole to learn the higher spiritual message. They recreate themselves by learning from their painful experiences.

Feeling the pain can actually transform your life, because it requires you to push through the knothole and once you exit—your life trajectory is altered. This alteration may have been the exact thing that was needed to place you on the path to your next assignment, your next lesson, and a reset. Without this painful experience you would have never made the shifts that were absolutely vital to get you to where you needed to be. These painful experiences are actually fuel that propels you to jump into the gap and begin to brew new possibilities. When you're living in possibility your living positively. When you're positive your energy, your light begins to rise and all those old painful experiences fall away and you begin to transcend the false illusions that you were wronged and replace it with the knowing that every struggle and challenge has a spiritual lesson. A spiritually reliable person will seek to understand and those who seek find. When someone who you care about hurts you, you can hold on to your anger, resentment and thoughts of revenge, or embrace forgiveness, seek to transcend and move up, forward and onward.

It is important for you to do the work it requires to make this upward leap. Meaning it may require you to seek outside counsel or coaching which will assist you in feeling and healing the wrong doing. As I have stated previously in order for you to heal, you must feel and when you feel you heal.

Nearly everyone has been hurt by the actions or words of another. Perhaps your mother criticized your parenting skills, your colleague sabotaged a project or your partner had an affair. These wounds can leave you with lasting feelings of anger, bitterness or even vengeance—but if you don't practice forgiveness, you might be the one who pays most dearly. By embracing forgiveness, you can also embrace peace, hope, gratitude and joy. Consider how forgiveness can lead you down the path of physical, emotional and spiritual well-being.

As I was writing this chapter my spiritual listening was activated and I was told very clearly to write this down on a post a note: "Find medical evidence on how not forgiving effects us physically, mentally, emotionally and spiritually." I remember thinking to myself, "Could there be documented evidence?" Being spiritually reliable I began the quest to find any medical documentation that could validate my intuitional claims. I stumbled upon a very validating article written by the Mayo Clinic labeling unforgivness as a physical, mental medical condition.

They share that letting go of grudges and bitterness can make way for compassion, kindness and peace. Forgiveness can lead to:

- Healthier relationships both with others and yourself.
- Greater spiritual and psychological well-being.
- Less anxiety, stress and hostility.
- Lower blood pressure.
- Fewer symptoms of depression.
- Lowers the risk of alcohol and substance abuse.[17]

For further reference I have included the full article in the appendix of this book.[18]

I feel the information written by the experts at the Mayo Clinic are spot on when medically labeling unforgivness as a significant factor contributing to the disharmony and diseases hiding in many peoples lives and bodies today.

My invitation for you would be to feel the pain as much as you need to feel it. But, understand the longer you hold on to the pain, agony and misery of any experience you are strapped down, held down by someone else's past acts. This causes your life force to be sucked out of you and you are unable to freely move about as a divine expression of God, as a Spiritually Reliable vessel. Or you can choose to be released from all and any past wrong doings, just by the mere claiming it as so, and by and in the authority of God's loving law. Shall we release this truth now into the law of God as Done? Yes! And, so it is!

Grounding Prayer

Dear God,
I acknowledge that I am always unified with your loving, everlasting energy. I choose to lie in the arms of divine flow, and give up my need to make others wrong. I decide now to let go of all grudges and bitterness of others whom I feel have said and done things to me, which hurt me. I reclaim my authority as a divine expression of God by letting go and forgiving others and myself. When I do forgive I know that only then can I freely move about in the world as a bursting expression of the divine spark that

was implanted in me at birth. I let go and forgive easily; I let go and allow God's grace to lift me up and over the resistance now. I release this prayer into the Law of God's as done. And, so it is.

Chapter 7: Spiritual Listening

When you learn how to spiritually listen you can then become Spiritually Reliable.

Each of us has God given gifts that were implanted in us at birth. These gifts are to be given, not withheld. When you deny your God given gifts and talents you are actually diminishing God's expression into the world. You actually appear smaller than you were programmed to be, so as a result you diminish your personal return. You must become brave enough to express your gifts or you will die with your gifts inside you. Your gifts are lying just below the surface, but you may have failed to quiet yourself in order for you to tap into them.

The very first step to living a spiritually reliable life is to learn to *listen spiritually.* You must discover how to calm your anxious mind to such a level that you can take notice of the divine whispers within. When you learn how to spiritually listen you can then become spiritually reliable.

Spiritually listening is paying attention to the inner voice within you; hushing your inner dialogue to such a level that you are able to hear all levels of knowing. You will then be willing to dance in the mystery of the unknown and release your attachment to the outcome by leaving your ego at the door. You are open to all you are hearing even when what you are hearing does not make sense to you.

Spiritual listening is an attribute of *being*, which is actually floating or being in neutral. When you are *being* there is nothing to do, except to *just be.* It is to be quiet, breathe, release, allow, and then be patient and wait on the small still voice within you to speak.

There are three levels at which we can hear the divine. We can hear *its* whispers in our heads, in our hearts and in our knowing. The headspace is a place where we process information such as numbers, ideas, directions, finances, and step-by-step instructions; it is a very worldly place. The heart space is a place where we process a connection to love, sympathy, devotion and empathy. The knowing is our gut space and is where we know that we know that we know; in this space we have an absolute clarity and calmness. I like to call this space the "Spiritual Spot." It is where our higher knowing resides and where our intuition is most vibrant and alive.

To become a spiritually reliable person we have to be aware of the three levels of knowing, and learn how to blend the three as one, because it takes all of our senses and human gifts to navigate this worldly experience— especially if you are one of the millions of people who are spiritually waking up and desiring to be of service in the world. Knowing this truth will support you as you walk into your spiritually reliable life.

There is a spiritual process, which has five steps that you can do to begin to learn how to become a reliable listener.

Step 1) Spiritual Quieting: For most people quieting their mind can be the most difficult task at hand, but this by far is the most important and necessary step to spiritual listening. Our minds are over stimulated living in the world. We are plugged into our phones all the time, and from the phone we can communicate with anyone we want.

You can begin by turning your phone, computers and TV's off and find a quiet space where you will not be bothered. Sit in a comfortable way that you can stay present and are relaxed. Begin taking in slow, controlled deep breaths—in and out. In through your nose, hold the breath, and then exhale the breath out your mouth, pushing out all the air from your lungs.

Continue to breathe in through the nose and out the mouth in the same slow, controlled way. Do this three to five times and once you begin to feel yourself still and quiet, begin watching the breath in your mind's eye. Visualize the breath as it moves through your body. See the breath as it moves into your mouth, throat, chest, and lungs; hold it deep in your stomach. Let yourself have a Buddha belly. Then watch the breath as it leaves your body, pushing out all stale air. Now, as you continue to breathe, start to scan your body for any place you are holding stress, tension, confusion or chaos. And, if you find that space within your body, simply breathe into that area. On the exhale, release it back into the universe to be recycled back for a greater higher good.

Now, once you know your body is quieting, begin to observe your inner thoughts—your inner dialog. Watch the thoughts pop up and then disappear as quickly as they arrive. Your thoughts are constant like clouds in the sky. Your thoughts float by, just as clouds do above you. Begin to be aware of your inner thoughts and when you begin to notice them, simply notice the thought and then come back to visualizing your breath. Visualize your breath moving in and out of your body. The power is in the visualization, so the more you visualize the more you use your subconscious mind. You are not visualizing if you are thinking. When you watch your breath move through your body, the act of doing so brings you fully into the present.

You now are ready to spiritually connect because you have quieted your body and mind.

Step 2) Spiritual Connecting: As I have stated numerous times throughout the book: You are never disconnected from God or your source. Having a restless and anxious mind makes feeling connected to source much more challenging. Anxious minds make having a clear connection to the divine far harder because it is like having static energy on the TV, and the way we dial into God's higher frequency is to have a clear, calm signal. Because you took the time to quiet yourself in the first step, you are now directly connected to the divine source. While you are listening to spirit's divinity, you must stay present to your mind. If your mind begins to disconnect and drifts into outer space and wanders away, you must call it back into focus.

Imagine it this way: Most of us have money in the bank and we use this bank to manage our finances. If you want to use the services of the bank you have to log into the system by going to an ATM machine or use your debit card to pay for your goods and services. The money is yours even when you are not tapping into it. In order for you to use your money, you have to tap into it by connecting to your bank's system. The bank is impartial if you use the money or not, just as God is impartial to whether you use its divine energy to support you or not, even if you are not connecting to God's loving energy in a moment of your life. God is like a wealthy bank, full of abundance streaming in at all times. All you have to do is learn how to log into its system properly and connect. When you do this you get a clean, clear, calm signal and then you can utilize its abundance.

Because you quieted yourself, you have now directly connected to source's signal and now you can begin to listen to what *it* is telling you.

Step 3) Spiritual Listening: The key to spiritual listening is to be in the mystery of the unknown and imagine yourself as an open channel for information to come and go. Pretend you are like a straw allowing fluid to move in and out of you. Always check yourself and make sure you are a clean, clear, open straw and not blocking the information by over processing what you hear. The headspace will want to understand what it is you hear; however, this is the quickest way to stop the fluidity of Spirit's voice. There is no time for heady thoughts in spirit's space.

Step 3 can be broken down into two types of *spiritual listening*:

1. Being the messenger for yourself.

2. Being the messenger for someone else.

Either way, we do not have to comprehend what it is we hear right now because these messages are seeds being planted to manifest in divine timing. It does not have to make sense to you in the exact moment you are hearing, feeling or seeing it because you are the vessel being utilized in this perfect moment; therefore, you know everything manifests in perfect divine order and perfect divine timing. You realize you are only the messenger and it only needs to make sense to the individual who is receiving the message. In order for me to remember this, I like to say to myself, "I am just being the messenger."

Step 4) Spiritual Courageousness: You have faith in the divine whispers you hear. You are brave, honest and loving with yourself and others, and you know that honesty without sensitivity is brutality. You walk as a spiritually reliable being with supreme faith in your connection with the divine and your faith is greater than your doubt. When you feel yourself hesitating, you ask for help from the many light beings who are willing to support you in being spiritually gutsy. Being spiritually courageous is realizing you cannot do it alone (no one does it alone), and you are willing to call out for spiritual direction when your faith is shaken.

A spiritually reliable person acknowledges the message as divine love, coming from a loving source and they allow the message to go where it needs to go in order for it to complete its cycle and journey. A spiritually reliable person knows it takes much bravery to stand up to the forces of this world. A spiritually reliable person knows that every encounter, every message is a divine appointment with another person, and they must be daring enough to speak, do, or go wherever spirit needs them next. This world is in spiritual warfare and without being spiritually courageous nothing will get done; nothing changes and more importantly the opportunities to be utilized for a greater, higher purpose are lost. We must be spiritually courageous and be brave to speak spirit's words when they arrive.

Step 5) Spiritual Reliability: Listening is only half of the equation. You must also be willing to take action when action is called for. "Listen only" mode will not move you or the world forward. Higher guidance can only guide if you allow it, and then you are the one who has to act with your body. To be spiritually reliable is the act of "doing" what it is you are seeing, sensing or hearing. It is acting with your body through doing, speaking and showing up for a greater higher purpose. It is knowing you are being utilized to do the work here and now. It is the act of serving and asking the question, "How may I serve?" and then acting with your life when you hear your higher knowing speak directly to you and through you. It is knowing you are the hands, voice, ears and feet in which the Universe does its work.

Sometimes being spiritually reliable is to pray and release—praying for love and light. It is not always about giving the person a message or helping them. You may be directed to just pray. In prayer we are actually co-creating with the Universal energy as a conduit for a certain outcome or praying within ourselves as an intercessor for the higher and greater good. Higher and greater good is not in your timing; it is all in divine timing. True intercession is when you know that the people cannot ask for themselves so you do it for them—to intercede on someone's behalf. However, in praying for others you must sometimes do it in confidentiality because people may take this in a negative way.

The key is to release the attachment to the outcome knowing the Universe has a plan for the person or situation. You may have a vision for the outcome, but who are you to do God's job? You should know that God can dream a bigger dream than you could possibly dream for them. Whatever it is you hear it is not yours to hold onto and you may not even remember what you said. Once you speak it or pray it out, it is theirs or God's to do what they choose. You are a vessel being utilized for a greater higher purpose. In doing so, you are a conduit allowing information to flow through you and not hold on to it. As my grandmother used to say, "A watched pot will never boil".

You are now co-creating your life with the most optimal presences available. I like to call this the dance among my mind, body and Spirit or you could refer to this phenomenon as being a Blended Being. I like to call this space the "Spiritual Spot". It is where our higher knowing resides and where our intuition is most vibrant and alive.

A while back I decided to use Facebook to learn how people hear spirit's voice. What I came to realize quickly is that beyond the process of spiritually listening, spirit's voice is alive and well in everything and everywhere. There is no place God, Universe, Spirit is not and *its* divine supreme energy is infused in everything. As I stated in the beginning of this chapter, "When you deny your God given gifts and talents you are actually diminishing Gods expression into the world." A singer singing, a speaker speaking, an actor acting, a dancer dancing, a teacher teaching, a minister preaching, a mom mothering, a cook cooking, a healer healing is God expressing itself through you. These and much more are all ways in which the Divine expresses itself through you. And, without your willingness, bravery and follow-through the divine's expression is thwarted and squashed. Here are a few examples of what others shared with me using Facebook to convey it. Yes, even Facebook is a place for the divine to express itself.

Q: How do you hear Spirit's voice? I Listen to Spirits voice by or through?

Amy: I get God bumps (goose bumps) in different places and different sensations. I pay attention for warnings and light bulb Ah-Ha's. As well as my dreams are pretty right on!

Laurie: Inner whispers and a weird feeling on the back of my neck—like a swoosh ...definitely through intuition.

Heather: Intuition and opportunity. If there's something I want to do, I've had times where everything in the universe seemed to align and all I had to do was show up. I've had other times where every door was locked and bolted. Oh, and don't forget the times when you just need to be detained for a few minutes. You'll lose your keys, look EVERYWHERE for 5-10 minutes and finally find them in their normal spot. When that happens, I've actually passed bad accidents that I probably would have been in if I hadn't been "late."

Katie: I am in the process of learning to listen to spirit, believe in spirit and discern when it's a source greater than myself. Sometimes I think I hear spirit, other times, I feel spirit-gut. Spirit can be a knowing or an external sign (usually repeated) and I'm observing that it tends to be Spirit when I don't like it :) Fear often tells me a more comfortable answer. Spirit definitely isn't found in my head!

Mike: It's a knowing that starts in my gut and spreads to my heart.

Rob: I hear Spirit's voice while listening to music.

I invite you to become present to how you hear spirit's voice. Pay attention to all the ways that spirit's voice is screaming out to you. Measure results by documenting each time you notice spirit speaking to you. Do this experiment for a few weeks and then look back at your results. I know you will become very aware of how spirit's voice is everywhere and seeking a divine connection with you.

Grounding Prayer

Dear God,
I now know when I learn how to spiritually listen;
I can then become spiritually reliable. I say yes
to claiming and learning how to integrate the
five steps to spiritual listening into my every day
life. I am willing to take time each day to quiet
my mind so I can hear the divine whisperings
moving through me and all around me. I do this
by creating space and time each day to close my
eyes, take in 5 deep slow controlled breaths and
allow myself to just be. I am the master of my
mind and let go of any anxious thoughts freely
and easily. From this calm state of mind I can
hear clearly and have a direct connection with
my higher self—my higher power. I listen, feel,
see and sense the divine messages burning
within me now. I act with graceful courage and
walk into the world as a spiritually reliable being.
I release this prayer into the Law of God as
done. And, so it is.

Chapter 8: Finding Purpose

We are all conduits for Spirit to move through us. Are you willing to be utilized for a greater higher purpose?

"How may I serve today?" This is a question that can create the most in your life. When you come from a place of service, you rapidly move into spirit's intention for the world. When you move into a service-oriented mind you co-create with universal law and begin doing spirit's work.

To find your purpose you must ask God to reveal it to you. God is not a person who sits on a Throne "up there." This presence is God, Universe, and Spirit or G.U.S. energy moving through you and all around you and you can call it all those words or none. Ask to be given a purpose that will serve and fulfill the highest and greatest good for all. When you do this you are stating that you are willing to serve as the highest expression of yourself, which will make it easier to live a spiritually reliable life.

Human beings are the manifestation of G.U.S. energy and are the moving machines that put spirit energy into action on earth. We are the hands, the ears and the eyes for spirit to use and create its grandest and most important earthly work; we are God's architects. G.U.S is always looking for people who are spiritually reliable and whom He can use to go out and do the work of righteousness. Willing, reliable humans are like God's puppets and He is the puppet master. The Universe will support you in your purpose because It made you to fulfill it.

Stop for a moment and think about this: When you ask the question of God, "How may I serve?" G.U.S. (God, Universe, Spirit) may answer with a small whisper inside you. It might be a quiet voice or it may come through another person or something you have read or heard. He may answer you with a more obvious answer, the answer you already knew but have been avoiding. To find your life purpose it requires you to pay attention to the signs, symbols and roadmaps. When you keep seeing certain messages and patterns reappearing, these are opportunities pointing you in the right direction. These things are subtle hints and clues from the universe guiding you to open doors and showing you the next step toward your life purpose. He will answer you in many different ways, but the point is that there is enough for everyone to do in this world and your job is to pay attention to the signs, symbols and roadmaps of life. Once you identify it by hearing, sensing, seeing, smelling or feeling it, go get it. This is how you become God's employee.

There are billions of needs in the world and God is looking for reliable workers to serve on this earth. When we work for God's purposes the phrase "free will" takes on an entirely whole new meaning. If you really think about it, do you really have free will when you work for God? Your will is being utilized by God for His purpose if you are committed to serving. If you allow your will to control the outcome, you might have the tendency to come from ego and then Edge God Out. An example of living from your ego could be:

What am I going to get from this?

God, Universe, Spirit is a doing machine, and does *its* doing through us. G.U.S. is always looking for people who are willing to do his work. The work is service to God and his purpose without attachment to the outcome. If we have any other agenda than to do God's work we come from a place of ego. Ego, which means – to Edge God Out, does exactly that, edges out God's purpose.

If you want to activate G.U.S, that which is the universal doing machine, you will need to ask the question, "How may I serve the world?" In that moment you are casting out a direct line to God's communication center, which then fulfills your request by sending you a message of how you can serve.

In this instant you must be obedient and able to spiritually listen to the inner voice within you. Be open to all you hear, see and feel. Allow yourself to sit in the stillness and just be with Gus's whispers, which delve inside you. What you hear in this stillness will lead you to your purpose.

Just like an employer who has hired you to do a job, G.U.S. will send you out into the world to serve, but only if you are 100% committed to the job and do what he needs you to do. Just as most employers, He prefers to send out those who are reliable and will show up with a positive and activated attitude.

If you stop and look around at the people who have done, or are doing spirit's great work, you can see that they all understood the concept of being a vessel and conduit for Spirit to move through them. Those people are just like you. They have human thoughts and, of course, they even have to battle with their egos and free will. Perhaps the difference between you and them is that they are willing to be utilized by spirit. They are reliable and God knows that He can trust their integrity and He knows that He is sending out a reliable C.A.R:

Clear – Available – Ready

- Clear—meaning you are clear with your intention to be a vessel and conduit for spirit to move through you without expectations or attachment to the outcome.
- Available—meaning you are open and willing to do what is asked of you by spirit without resisting, and you are not coming from a place of "what am I going to get from this?"
- Ready—meaning you are ready to serve spirit's purpose for your life and the life of others that are in

need and have come to you for help or counsel. You have a "show up" activated attitude.

Car's listen and respond to God's call from a neutral place. Cars are willing to be egoless, selfless and serve the world from a place of spiritual enlightenment and alignment. They choose a higher vibration in which they connect to God's purpose. From that place they move into the flow of goodness and begin to serve the world from a selfless and powerful place producing joy, love and acceptance in a world of a billion needs.

Everyone can find a purpose, but not everyone can find a *high level* purpose. A high level purpose is one that serves the greater higher good of all. It is an extension of God's love into the world. For example, I could have a goal to write a book and make millions of dollars and become famous. Or I could write a book with a high level intention to reach more and more people in the world, helping them to have better lives. Which one do you think would serve the greater higher good of all?

Co-creating your purpose with your higher power will ultimately lead you to your high level purpose. A high level purpose is doing something that brings added value to the people's lives you serve. It consists of up leveling and taking you and those you serve to a better place. When you do this you are living in a higher vibrational space of service, gratitude, and living a purpose-driven life.

We ask ourselves at times, "Why am I here?" And, some of us do not know how to answer the question. In Richard Bach's book, *Illusions*, he says, "Here is a test of whether or not your mission in life is finished. If we are alive it isn't." To make changes in your life you have to wake up to the awareness that you are not living fully to your potential. To experience life fully is to realize your life purpose or calling— the reason we are here on earth.

One way to find your mission in life is to become aware of when you feel blissful. Do you remember a time when you were doing something for many hours and when you looked at the clock you realized time flew by? This is what I like to call bliss, where time does not exist. To find your bliss ask yourself, where does time not exist? This is where you belong. Listen for it by becoming aware of the loss of time.

Try new things that show up in your life. If you always go back to what you know you will never expand enough to find your bliss. There is always something you can create to help find bliss. Take a risk and move out of your comfort zone. Become aware of the types of things to which you are attracted. Move toward those things; start doing them and watch yourself become alive with a constant stream of endurance and abundance that is going directly into what you are creating. Now, you are co-creating with God and His purpose for you on earth. Become a doer of what you do really well and what comes naturally to you. When you realize what you are doing is enjoyable and you do not mind putting forth the effort to do it because it seems effortless, then you are in your bliss.

You are not an extra; there are no extra human beings. You have a purpose that is full, abundant and will leave you feeling complete at the end of your day. You can move effortlessly into the world with a purpose when you are clear, available and ready.

1. Clear with your intentions and let go of your personal expectation and attachment to the outcome.
2. Clear that God can dream a bigger dream than you can dream for yourself.
3. You are available to serve spirit's needs without resistance and are not coming from a place of, "What am I going to get from this?"
4. Ready with a show up and activated attitude.

Grounding Prayer

Dear God,
Help me find my purpose in life. I know when I
show up as a spiritually reliable vessel I am
happy because I am glorifying you. May I walk
into my life's purpose aware of each footstep I
take. May I take one step at a time into my life's
purpose, my bliss. You are calling me by name. I
give thanks for the knowledge; I am worthy of a
purpose and the timeless void of bliss. I release
this prayer into the Law of God as done. And, so
it is.

Chapter 9: Be Here Now

Right now is all there is, everything else is an illusion.

Throughout the years, many authors have written about the concept of "Now" and there are many ideas of what the power of now is. Living in the now is all we have; therefore, everything else in an illusion. Living a spiritually reliable life commits us to the Divine plan even though we can forecast our future, set goals and deadlines. There are two types of plans: Your plan and God's plan. God can dream a bigger dream than you can dream for yourself. If this were true, then would it not be more proactive to live in the present moment and create from there?

Many people struggle with living in the now, and when you fluctuate, staying present to what is happening now becomes difficult. You are usually in one of two places: You are either in your past or your future, and quite frankly neither of those "spaces" is real. What I like to say is that you're just hallucinating.

We create obstacles to living a spiritually reliable life when we live in any other place *but* in our current moments. When you are in thought about your past or future, the divine cannot use this mind to create in the now. The mind that lives in past or future is a mind that is anxious, and the divine is unable to tap into such a mind. A spiritually reliable being is someone who can show up in the current moment and be clear, available and ready. When we drag in our pasts or spend too much energy focused on our future, then how can we be clear, ready and available to receive our next message or hear our next mission?

Imagine moving through your day believing you are right where you are supposed to be at any given moment. You follow the intent and direction God wants for you. God has given you visions of your life, and if you just stop for a moment and reflect, you will remember a time when you had this knowing revealed to you. The knowing was God showing you a vision. This vision may be revealed to you through a thought, another person's words, a book, a movie, a song, and a dream, or in many multitudes of ways. The knowing is within you. You know it, now how do you master it?

Take on one task at a time. Follow God's path and allow God to create your future. Speak your intention out loud because intention is everything. Without intention we are wandering around without a plan. Ask God to help you be of service. "How may I serve today? I say yes to my life today." Be grateful for this experience being alive and enjoying this moment.

Time slips away very quickly and then it becomes your past. Ahead of you is the future, and the past is slipping away just as quickly as the future arrives. Both are fully present, occurring simultaneously. It is time overlapping time, moving through you and in you. When we are all living in the now, each one of us will be in complete awareness, as a fully realized being. This is all you have and all you should be grateful for in this moment of now.

Ride the moment of now by catching the momentum like you are catching a wave in the ocean. Let it guide you like gravity guides the tides. The pull and tug of the current is God riding you like a jockey rides a thoroughbred racing horse. The jockey guides the horse through pulling, tugging, plowing and using certain amounts of pressure. Let God ride you in the race of your life. Run like the wind, kick up your heels, lift your tail and let your mane flap in the wind.

Living in the now and allowing God to create your day involves letting go and letting God. When you put yourself in neutral and wait on God's whispers within you, he will tug on your heart and move you in a certain direction. When you listen closely to the whispers, they will remind you of who you are and who you have come here to be. When you serve others in the now, you are the hands, ears, feet and voice creating new evolving thoughts and concepts. Being in the now is the only place that is real.

Have you ever taken a vacation where everything was planned? You knew what time you would arrive, where you were going to eat, all the activities you were going to do. There was a sense of social obligation and there was no freedom to be impulsive and allow the day to unfold. Something tugging on you, begging you to step out of your planned agenda can make those types of trips frustrating. You may have stood on a street corner and noticed something down the street that looked really fun or inviting. But, because you already had everything planned for the day and were socially obligated, you felt like you couldn't do what your heart wanted to do. Not having preplanned trips are the best ones. All you know is the destination, when you are going to leave and when you will return. Everything else in between is up to spirit to guide you and ride you through those trips. The most rewarding and fulfilling trips are the ones where you see yourself as a leaf in the wind. The power is in the now. Now is all you have. You can forecast the future and have goals to achieve, but ultimately it's up to God.

A previous client of mine once took a nine-day cruise to the Mexican Riviera. Each day he would awaken with no expectations. He never knew what he would feel like doing that day. He remained open to whatever the universe had in store for him. He reported that the vacation was amazing and was everything he needed; he was spontaneous and in the moment of now. When he returned home he found there was completeness within himself and he had no regrets.

I remember a story I heard one day on the local news that put it all into perspective. There was a bus full of people. I am sure each person woke up in the morning with a plan, places to go and things to achieve for the day. Well, none of those passengers with a plan made it to their destinations. A gun-slinging madman hijacked the bus. Just as the bus was traveling over a bridge, this man shot the bus driver sending the bus flying off the bridge to an apartment complex below. Many people in the bus died, including the bus driver and the man who hijacked the bus. Some of the people below were also hurt and killed, and their plans for the day were ultimately thwarted as well.

Living in the now, and its importance, makes this story a perfect example. Of course we have places to be and things to do, but if God wants to change those plans He does in an instant. When we release, let go and let God we are allowing Spirit to move through us and to create our day. Tragic events occur each and every day. There is a reason for each one of them. The best thing we can do is to go with the flow and know there is a reason, even if we do not understand what the reason is.

Grounding Prayer

Dear God,
Help me to understand the things that do not
make sense to me. I live in the now and let go of
all my worries about my past or my future. I
know when I lay awake at night worrying that I
am not living in the now. I say yes to a still mind
and I let my mind be clear, available and ready. I
know when I let go I will know. I release this
prayer into the Law of God as done. And, so it is.

Chapter 10: Stretching

When God is your employer he sometimes takes you to places that push you to your physical, mental, emotional and spiritual limits. This is evolving.

Another way we struggle living a spiritually reliable life is when we do not embrace the awkward feelings of stretching ourselves. Being willing to stretch yourself into uncomfortable is necessary in order for you to live a life of wholeness, fullness and completeness. When we are the most uncomfortable in our lives, it really is a time that we are growing and reaching further than we have ever reached before. Growing is uncomfortable, but absolutely imperative if we want to expand ourselves. Without moments of uncomfortable, we do not really live to our truest and highest potentials.

I once received an email from a client who did Bikram hot yoga, or as he labeled it, "Nazi Yoga." He referred to it that way because most of the time he would be very uncomfortable in class. He shared that the room was always over 100 degrees. There were 27 postures where he was instructed to hold for certain amounts of time and then repeat them. The teacher was relentless in insisting he hold the postures flawlessly under what seemed like overwhelming pressure. The point of each posture was to hold each one perfectly so he could get the benefit of each one. Yes, sometimes it was very challenging and difficult, and each class would push him to his mental and physical limits.

What yoga taught him was that he had to deal with his body's sensations and feelings. He learned to sit in the fire—sit in the burn and feel his feelings and just be with them. He would have to calm his mind down and breathe into whatever sensation he was feeling. His mind would start telling him stories like: "Oh my God, I can't hold this posture any longer. It is too hot in here. I wish I had not come today. How much longer?"

The benefits were best felt when he could hold the posture perfectly and stay in the right state of mind. When he avoided the perfect posture, the perfect hold, then he was not stretching himself to evolve into a more complete person. When the going was tough it was usually because he was allowing his own mind to drive his practice.

When you allow yourself to sit inside the sensation of your feelings—pains and emotions—you stretch and evolve to a level that has true holistic benefits. Within the hold and stretch comes satisfaction, and only then will your soul and body connect to a higher level of being.

We, as humans, are evolving creatures. To achieve our highest and best self we must stretch and push forward. When we resist something it is usually a clue that we really need to move deeper into what we are trying to avoid. When we avoid something it only delays our soul's expression of who we are meant to be. When we avoid a posture or mindset we are really delaying our own peace, happiness, joy, fulfillment, and greatness.

When we are uncomfortable with our lives it is our greatest awareness that we are stretching, evolving and growing. Without feeling discomfort we do not grow into the people we are meant to be. Embrace the awkwardness of strange feelings and postures that put you into a place of discomfort because only then do you move forward, change and grow into a deeper and more fulfilled person.

Stretching is never comfortable, and in yoga we learn that when you feel the stretch to the point you think you're going to break, all you need to do is take a deep breath and exhale even deeper. We can apply this to our non-yoga lives and stretch ourselves to feel uncomfortable. From the breath we then can move more deeply into the postures of our lives. From each breath we gain an inner knowing we can move deeper and more fully into the life we were created to have.

Breathe deeply and exhale even deeper. Move, evolve, grow and expand. It's all part of God's plan.

Grounding Prayer

Dear God,
Help me to realize that when I am the most
uncomfortable in my life, it only means I am
expanding, growing and evolving. I know
stretching is never easy and sometimes it hurts.
I know now when I believe in myself and allow
myself to breathe deeply into the places that
stretch me the most, I will push forward and out
of things that challenge me the most. I sit inside
the fire today in pure and absolute faith knowing
there is relief just through the breath. I release
this prayer into the Law of God as done. And, so
it is.

Chapter 11: Hold It Up To The Light

All conflict, drama, disagreements, and detachments can be held into the light.

Another way we create limits to living a spiritually reliable life is when we do not hold our conflicts and disagreements with others into the light. For the purposes of my teachings, holding something up to light means to expose or reveal the truth about something and to bring clarity to a situation.

A conflict or disconnect with anything you experience as drama is full of darkness and low light illusions. Imagine if you could see the presence of a conflict as a great wise teacher; showing up and allowing you to experience something to serve your greater, higher good, pushing and evolving you and the other person(s) to a new place, a shift, a seed of growth. Imagine if you were to invite the conflict in for a conversation. Imagine this situation is helping you and guiding you where you need to be in your life. It is ultimately a shift in perception from fear to love. Then, release it by knowing and claiming that everything is in divine timing and divine order.

Let me paint a metaphorical picture: Let's

imagine that you are unloading the dishwasher full of dishes that were just washed. You get to thinking that maybe the dishes are not quite clean enough. What is the first thing you do? You hold the glass up to the light to see through it clearly. By holding the glass up and into the light above, you see if it is really clean, smudged, filmy, or just needs to be rinsed.

Imagine that this is how you approach any conflict you are experiencing in your life. Obviously this is metaphorical in nature and you cannot literally hold up your fight with your spouse into the light. But, you can decide to hold the situation up to God in order for the truth to be revealed. You can ask this simple question:

How can I apply love here?

When you ask such a profound question as, "How can I apply love here?" you are holding the conflict up to the light and then you are able to see through it clearly. It then quickly becomes egoless. Your awareness goes immediately to a higher thought and higher vibration. You are then able to clearly see the bigger picture, a bird's eye view of the truth.

With the conflict defused and unarmed, you simply shift into forgiveness and right thinking. You tap into the magical dance of choosing love. The magic is a simple shift in perception from blaming, then to asking, to seeing the highest truth. By pausing and leaning in to listen, you hear the higher truth. You then begin to attract the message with ease because you ask to see it—shifting you into a higher vibration and raising your energy to vibrate at the same level as your desires.

When we go from blaming, struggling, isolating, shaming, and judging to asking for the spiritual lesson to be revealed, we make the shift from fear to love and then the magical dance of miracles takes form within you. Choosing to stand in the light will help keep the situation where the light is. It is ultimately a shift in perception from fear to love. You are choosing peace as opposed to being right.

Every person experiences conflict in his or her life. This is a part of your journey. And most conflicts stem from disagreements with others. Every experience, every struggle could be reframed. You can call it fear, obstacle, conflict, confusion or drama. Or, you could call it in for an interview and an opportunity for your growth. God is not invested in the details of your situation. God is invested in your spiritual enlightenment.

A Course in Miracles says, "The relationship is the classroom for the Holy Spirit."[19]

What this means is that without relationships in our lives we do not grow or evolve. This human journey is about having relationships. We all need them because we all need to evolve into the highest best expression of ourselves. When conflicts show up in our lives we have an opportunity to grow into our highest, best selves. In order for this to happen we must ask for help in this moment. We must ask for the truth to be revealed. Just as it is written in Mathew 7:7, "Ask, and it shall be given to you; seek, and you shall find; knock, and it shall be opened for you, for every one that asks shall receive; and he that seeks will find; and if you knock it shall be opened."[20]

I remember when my grandmother passed away in 2005. As Nana was dying I had one last conversation with her before she left her human suit. It was super late in the evening as I sat next to her bed. I was the only person in the room, and she woke up after being asleep for a very long time. She looked at me and asked me why the garage door was open? I was perplexed because the curtains were drawn and it was 1:00 a.m. I thought to myself, "How does she know if the garage door is open?" I stood up and looked out the window and sure enough the garage door was wide open. She had not left the bed for four days before this and there would be no way she could have known this to be true or not. I told her I would go shut it after I left her room. I knew in this moment she was dancing between two worlds, the human world and the other side. I sat back down near her and she just stared at me. I asked her if she wanted to talk. She replied, "No, I have nothing to say. Do you want to ask me something?" I could tell this was a defining moment because something about her felt different, she seemed softer to me. I replied with this question, "Nana what do you remember about your life?"

"I remember when I loved and when I was loved."

I can still remember the impact that simple sentence left on me. How simple and yet how powerful, I thought. I could feel the level of absolute truth in these simple words. We must remember that to live a spiritually reliable life we must give love and be willing to receive love.

You have to understand my grandmother was an 80 year old, very fiery, stubborn, bull headed, woman who probably did not hold many conflicts up to the light. In the end she shared with me how she loved and how she was loved. Nana broke it down to the purest essence of all spiritual laws. When her body became sick and she was left with only her soul's essence, it was as if she could finally soften into the truth about life.

In the end she could have remembered much, much more. She could have remembered the times in her life when she was hurt, rejected, abused, divorced, sick, or even the happy times. But, what she remembered was love. Loving others and being loved by others. When she was alive in her healthy body she held a lot of resentment towards others, unwillingness to forgive. Being the stubborn woman she was, she would never forget if you ever did her wrong.

Is it possible she left this world knowing the truth, knowing the meaning of life? I have to believe it is so. Ironically, these were her very last words she ever spoke to me. In the end, she found absolute perfection. Nana's last words have now become my anchor in life. Whenever you feel yourself having the need to be right or make others wrong, remember the only thing that is real is love and everything else is an illusion. Filter yourself by asking this question:

How can I apply love here?

When you ask this question you are aligning yourself with the One mind, God's mind, Universal loving mind. When you choose love, the veil of uprightness is removed and your lenses completely clear. You no longer see anger or hatred. You no longer want to control others and make them see your ideas as correct. You choose to let people believe what they want to believe, choose what they choose, experience what they will experience and know in the end your job is to apply love in every situation you can. When you do, life becomes easy.

People will get to their own epiphanies, realizations and their own truths in divine timing, not our timing and not your timing. The only real thing we can do is to allow people to be where they are. When we try to fix, rescue and help the unwilling we really only handicap them further. To fully grasp what the lesson is to be learned, sometimes people need to fall down on their own.

The Horse Whisperer is one of my favorite movies. In the movie, Tom is a well-known horse trainer and people knew him as the horse whisperer. He was given a horse that was assumed to be not trainable. When Tom showed up at his ranch, the men who hired him to train the horse expected Tom to corral, lasso and force the horse into submission. But, instead he ignored the horse and didn't pay the horse any attention. Each day Tom would show up at the corral where the horse was being kept and would just hang out and do nothing. Day by day he would creep in a little closer, and slowly begin to integrate himself into the horse's space. Tom would get just close enough so that the horse knew he was there, and then Tom would turn around to leave and ignore the horse. He repeated the process day in and day out.

One day Tom became frustrated with the process and about to give up and started believing that the horse was not trainable. But, in his heart he knew the truth about the horse's experience. He held the horse into the light and revealed the truth. The horse did not trust people and had many bad experiences. He knew the horse had come from a world of abuse and had been forced into doing things that the horse was not ready to do. The horse had never seen a loving human before and therefore, did not trust. This was why the horse was so unwilling to serve.

Tom slowly moved into the horse's space, then turned around, ignored the horse and waited. He waited hours, sitting down on the ground in the middle of the corral with his back turned towards the horse. Hours went by until slowly a miracle began to take place. The horse began to creep slowly closer and closer to Tom until he finally placed his muzzle on Tom's shoulder and submitted.

Tom saw the horse's potential but was spiritually smart enough to know not to grab, tug or pull on the horse because those behaviors do not demonstrate love. The horse was not ready and was on his own timeline. Tom decided to see through the eyes of love and apply love to the horse's situation. He knew that the horse was built to work, submit and serve. But, because the horse experienced unloving experiences the horse was unwilling to love back. In this situation the horse whisperer applied love and in the end love prevailed.[21]

There is a place for all conflict, drama, disagreements and detachments to be held up to the light. No matter what you experience in your life, apply love to all situations, and the fog will be lifted and you will see clearly. Applying love is the answer for all problems.

Grounding Prayer

Dear God,
Please take away my unloving thoughts and
beliefs about life. I am willing to apply love in
every situation I encounter. I know that every
conflict or disagreement is an opportunity to
grow into my highest, best self. I am willing to
hold all struggles into the light for the greater
higher purpose of seeing the truth. I let go of my
resistance and receive love today. I release this
prayer into the Law of God as done. And, so it is.

Chapter 12: Mind the Gap

If you're not where you were and you're not where you want to be, you are in between, inside the Gap, the gap of possibility.

Another way we scuffle with living a spiritually reliable life is when you do not embrace the gaps of your life and instead choose to resist them. The definition of a gap is: you're not where you were and you're not where you want to be, you are in between, in a space of uncertainty.

When you resist these gaps you actually dim your own life force by delaying the experience of walking your divine path. Your job as a spiritually reliable being is to become familiar with what a gap is and most importantly, learn how to navigate the gaps of your life because gaps are just apart of life.

Many people come to seek counsel from me, and many who come are facing a dilemma in their lives, in which they feel out of control and unable to move forward. They all come with the same paralyzing fear that is moving through them, with their stories always being different but somewhat familiar to me. They are all in a haze of uncertainty, each soul is resisting, struggling for understanding, and wanting to learn how to navigate this foggy gap of ambiguity.

As I sit with my clients and hold a sacred

space for them to share their stories with me, I have a bodily sensation of joy bubbling up within me. I know this sacred soul before me is shifting, changing, healing, stretching and most importantly evolving to a higher and different level from where they were. They are going through a space of time, which I call the Gap. Gap stands for "God's Automatic Purge." I congratulate these people because they are shifting into a new normal and purging what is no longer serving them.

In this moment of time in the gap, you might feel a sense of overwhelm to the point of never knowing how you're going to move through this and make it to the other side unscathed, still alive, without losing all the things you have worked so hard to obtain. There could be a paralyzing fear, which has the potential of totally derailing you into a place of depression and anxiety, leaving you completely wrecked and unable to move on with your life. The doom comes in like a wild winter storm taking away all visibility and leaving you with a blinded sense of perception. Letting doubt and fear enter into your mind is creating the most negative outcomes opposed to positive outcomes. Doubt is the enemy because it feeds the ego the most perfectly measured meal to continue to survive and feed off of your fear based emotions. To me, doubt means, "Digging out uncertainty blindly threatening your faith."

Spiritually reliable people understand the divine laws behind the three D's: details, delays and detainment. They know there are blocking angels, and they know there are angels whose job it is to open doors. These angelic deities work for G.U.S. (God, Universe, Spirit) on behalf of all humanity and work for our greater higher good. Spiritually reliable people have more faith in the supreme beings above than they do doubt. Spiritually reliable people know that G.U.S can see more than we see, and are willing to be obedient to the divine eye in the sky.

Every person has been in a gap in his or her life before. Most of us forget the extreme paralyzing fear we experienced then because we've moved on and gotten through it. We all have times when we were in a gap and somehow it all worked itself out. This is where your faith comes into play. This is where you have to remind yourself that there have been trying times before and somehow you were able to get through it and handle it. This is when you have to walk into the gap with blind faith knowing you will move through this in perfect order, perfect timing.

When you are in the gap it will probably be a very uncomfortable place to stand. Fortunately, when you are uncomfortable it only means you are stretching and growing to a new level of life. Those who do not embrace these awkward moments and sensations cannot grow further. It can be easy to lose perspective of what is really happening and begin to spin out of control. Seeing the big picture can be very hard to visualize because in this time you are anchored in the middle of the river not knowing if you should go left or right.

Sometimes when you are inside the gap, the world of effects can spin around you causing you to feel unstable, uncertain and scared. In these moments you must learn how to calm your mind, be quiet, ask for guidance, listen, and breathe. Repeat this mantra to ground you and anchor you in these stormy seas:

The center of who I am is indestructible.

The world of effects is always spinning around you without interruption, but it is your job to stay in your center, and when you do, nothing can knock you off balance. Wait on God's still voice within you, the center of who you are to nudge you, to move you forward. Remind yourself that everything is in divine timing and you have no control, except how you choose to see things. Surrender and connect to your faith and remember this too will pass because no storm will last forever.

It is not your job to worry about the when, where or how. The universe is all knowing, all doing and does not need to know your details. If you want to build a rose garden, just say yes to building a rose garden; don't clog the universal doing machine with all of your details. The universe already knows your hearts desire; it will take care of you, and all the details. The only thing you need to do is say yes to your life, say yes to your divine plan and then wait on divine timing to unfold beneath you. If you want to build a rose garden, then clearly state this. Do not bog down the universe by over processing the details. When you say yes to building a rose garden, the universe hears your request and goes into action for you. You do not need to worry about the hose, trellis, gloves, roses, shovel or fertilizer because the only thing the universe needs to know is that you say yes to building a rose garden. G.U.S. already knows you need all those things to build a beautiful garden and when you get too specific you clog the divine eye in the sky with too many details.

The universe looks back at you and says, "I am God, but I am confused by your request. I am not sure if I should give you the hose, trellis, gloves, roses, shovel or fertilizer, because all I need to know is that you say yes to building a rose garden. I already know all the details to building a rose garden; leave the rest up to me." The details to building a rose garden are in Divine timing; not you're timing.

God is a doing machine and only knows to do what you tell it to do. As stated previously, God can dream a bigger dream than you can dream for yourself. Sometimes these gaps and delays of time are actually designed by the divine for your greater higher good and are there to propel you into a brand new trajectory. These gaps will put you on a new life path; a path filled with purpose, power, passion and a plan.

God's delays do not always mean God's denial. The eye in the sky, the universal source moving through you and all around you knows you intimately. God knows that you can sometimes desire to manifest worldly possessions, relationships, jobs, and many other worldly possibilities that are not always for your greater higher good. You can manifest anything you desire, both at the low level and high level of life. God is all knowing, all seeing. He is perched up in consciousness and embodies clear seeing from the vastest, widest, global perspective of any consciousness. And when you desire those things, experiences that are not for your greatest and highest good, you are placed in a time out, a holding space, a gap.

I compare it to a child wandering into unsafe territory; yes the territory is there for you to experience – one day, but not now. Yes, this space may be safe for others to venture into, but for you, it is not your divine path to experience yet. We sometimes have to barricade spaces off in our homes to keep the children from hurting themselves. God will barricade many people from many paths, and many doors do not open for us because there is a divine plan and with that comes divine timing. Could you reframe locked doors, gaps of time, details, delays and detainments as a divine time out? These gaps are delivering you unto your divine order and a certainty that only God could possibly dream for you.

A spiritually reliable person knows that everything happens when it is supposed to happen, and when you jump into the Gap—God catches you. Yes, you can force things into reality, but how many times have you forced something to manifest and only later realize that it wasn't best for you? When you are driving, pushing and twisting things into happening you are not living a spiritually reliable life because you are pushing against divine order. Spirit comes to us with a clear knowing, a gut of truth, a whisper, and sometimes a loud crash when you're not listening. In no way am I saying to resign and to just wait for the universe to hand you your next assignment. I am telling you to pay attention, ask for higher guidance to deliver you to the right moment, the perfect opportunities where your God given gifts and talents may be utilized for the greater higher good of all. When you state such a high level intention externally or internally, spirit hears your order and moves towards you and begins to orchestrate all the details to accommodate your requests; but only when your intentions are pure, and come from a high level space to serve. Once you do hear the voice of God, it is now your job to show up where you have been guided to be next and wait on the divine to give you your next task to move you forward.

The Gap is a reset taking you from one place to another. It is a time to up level your life. Gaps can sometimes be dull and painstakingly annoying because you're in a holding pattern waiting for divine timing to arrive. In order for God to get you to where you need to be next, He sometimes has to rip the rug out from underneath you and shake up your reality.

Jumping into the Gap requires you to TRUST:

- **Trust & Allow**
- **Release & Accept**
- **Understand with Faith**
- **Surrender & Release**
- **Transcend**

It is simply summed up as, "Trust the process." You should know that in all actuality you would never leave the gap permanently; you just slide from one gap to the next. Being in the gap is a part of life. We are always waiting for something to change, shift, be over, move, be done with, start or begin; it will never end. The key is to embrace this "space" and realize it is all a part of God's perfect plan for your life. When you let go and let the gap, the space in between reveal its lessons, the mystery becomes mystical. Gap is faith, and faith is moving into the unknown, stepping in and knowing that where you're being called is beyond your wildest dreams. Do not fear the leap of faith— the jump into the gap, because this is the only way you can grow. With thoughts of fear and doubt you develop "Dis-ease", meaning you disconnect from your divine path, and in turn put disease into your life. God designed us to always evolve; you and I are built to endure and withstand.

Everyone's life must shift and change from

time to time; otherwise we become complacent. The dictionary defines complacency as: a feeling of quiet pleasure or security, often while unaware of some potential danger, defect, or the like, self-satisfaction or smug satisfaction with an existing situation or condition. What rings true for me in this definition is, "unaware of some potential danger, defect or the like." I define complacency as a slow death to your soul. You are anesthetized and unaware of the fact that there might be another choice besides your current reality. A slow death to the soul would for sure be something with potential threat. The key is to have awareness when you are going complacent in your life. Without the awareness, it sneaks up on you and eventually demeans you. Many people get stuck in a rut, a routine without even realizing they are in a rut, and are numb to any other reality beyond the one they know. This spot can be comfortable or uncomfortable depending on how aware you are. Some people decide to revolve in their life and some people decide to evolve their life.

I remember hearing a story from a woman who was seated next to me on a plane. Planes have a strange way of getting you or those sitting next to you to share personal details with strangers. She shared that she had been in a relationship with the same person for many years and it had become very comfortable, but she felt like she was dying inside and was just going through the daily motions. She did the same things day in and day out for many years.

Then one day a part of her soul began to awaken and realize, that her reality could be different. She told me she had a pull within her that said, "You want more than just this, you need to have more experiences in the world, see the world, and contribute to making a difference in the world." She knew she wanted something more, but was not exactly sure what it was she wanted.

This nudge, pull, tug and awareness is a potential catalyst shifting your reality. When you pay attention to these signs you then become a spiritual listener; wake and begin to prepare yourself to jump into the gap. Apart from preparing to jump, you need to decide what you will do with this pull from within. Deciding something new can be very scary because it might not just affect you, but it can also affect everyone around you. The people in your life get stuck in how they see you and what role you play in their lives. When you decide to shift into something new it has the potential of creating a chain reaction all around you.

Metaphorically it is like a tremor or earthquake in your life and the people in your life feel it. You might want to change and the people who say they want to support you hang on to the way you were. This is a very dangerous place for some because you are seeing something new within yourself, you are seeing the change as a part of your own self-evolution, but the people in your life are clinging for this change to stop because your shift is making them shift.

However, you must be willing to embrace the idea that you are programmed naturally to self evolve. Your spirit and soul have a desire to reach further, explore deeper and when those shifts happen it brings up a lot of fear from others around you and is the reason for their lack of support. You may find that friends or family tell you they support your changes, but then down the road they may begin to start trying to talk you out of your dreams because they don't see what you see. They are afraid of losing the old you to the new you. Could it be that they are resisting themselves and not allowing their own internal self-evolving programming to develop further? Spiritually reliable vessels know the moment you step into your spiritual path the universe will begin to change your thoughts, clear your vision, and open doors to truths that were beyond your wildest dreams. But, not all people will have these experiences or realizations; therefore they cannot understand your perceptions of the world. These are very awkward moments in our lives and it is like we are being pushed through a knothole and no knothole is a straight shot to the other side. These moments are forcing you and those in your life to jump into the gap of the unknown – pushing your consciousness to mind the gap.

In London, on the underground, every time the doors open to the trains, an automated voice repeats "MIND THE GAP." It is a London catchphrase, but more of a reminder to pay attention to what's going on around you and watch where you're stepping. When people are commuting, touring or traveling, there is a gentle reminder that there is a space in between that can bring you awareness to your current position and moment. It reminds you to arrive in the now and pay attention or you may fall into the gap and hurt yourself. If you don't mind the gap, then you're not minding the miracles.

See all gaps, delays and detainments as spaces and places where new possibilities develop, but always hold the vision and trust the process. The gaps of your life are the places that are transporting you to the next level of your life; but of course as T.S. Eliot said, "We shall not cease from exploration and at the end of all our exploring, will be to arrive where we started and know the place for the first time."[22]

To live a spiritually reliable life you must be willing to mind the gap and to see all delays, as a holding pattern that you have been put into before it's time to land at your next assignment. These life gaps are your greatest and wisest teachers when you settle down with them and ask them to reveal their many truths. Spiritually reliable people embrace and see all delays as having a divine purpose and more importantly— Spiritual lessons. Hold the vision, trust the process, trust the divine plan, and know that everything is in divine order; everything is just as it should be.

Are you minding the gap? Is your faith greater than your doubt when you are in the gap? Are you willing to trust the gap and to know you are being divinely ushered into new spaces of possibility? How Divine!

Grounding Prayer

Dear God,
I now know that delays do not always mean denial. I understand that the gaps of time I am in from time to time are actually holding patterns protecting me, supporting me, loving me and bringing me to spaces and places where I can become the highest expression of myself. I know that gaps are designed to corral me, to reset me and to support me on my divine path. I am now willing to trust the process and know that God can dream a bigger dream that I could possibly dream for myself. I embrace the gaps and see them as places to slow down, reset, and wait on the Divine to open the door. I know everything is in divine timing and I am a part of the master plan. I release this prayer into the Law of God as done. And, so it is.

Chapter 13: Spiritual Lessons

A tragedy can turn out to be our greatest good if we approach it in ways from which we can grow.
—Louise Hay[23]

Another way you can struggle with living a spiritually reliable life is when you do not embrace all challenges as your greatest, wisest teachers that have come to teach something very important. A spiritually reliable person has a deep knowing within them that there are no accidents, only lessons. They choose to live in the possibilities and know there is magic in all misfortune. They stop to ground themselves, assess the situation and ask for the spiritual lessons to be revealed. The high amount of awareness needed in this moment is beyond transformational. However, by asking for the spiritual lessons to be revealed, you are demonstrating that you are ready for the adventure of revelation, resolution and resurrection. You can do this by making the connection with your higher power and remembering that all problems stem from separation. Therefore, the solution comes through connection.

You must learn to connect daily with a power greater than yourself. By immersing yourself into this magnificent powerhouse you are reaching into a source that has unbelievable strength and resources with the ability to fully support you. For me, I call this power God. By consciously making this connection you are surrendering to the truth that you, yes you, need help. A spiritually reliable person knows that they cannot do this alone; they know that no one can do this alone. They possess the understanding that all human beings need divine guidance and help.

Many people believe you must pray, beg and cry for help from God. You can certainly pray, and prayer works, but I know an easier way: Instead of praying in a way that you are begging and crying for help and using diminishing words like, "I hope, I wish, I'll just get by, I just want enough to survive," become powerful in your words and choose to use words that are powerful and will increase you. Invite God into your life; invite His angels into your life to intervene and bring you more. These angels are capable of handling any of your earthly dilemmas because they are messengers, or mediaries who unite in your life for your greatest and highest good. They travel between you and God's divine intelligence center. Everyone has angels assigned to him or her, and yours are waiting with baited breath to support you. They are literally hovering around you at all times and your job is to simply invite them to intervene with your life. Remember that neither God nor his angels have the power to take away your free will, so you must invite them in. A mistake many people can make is when they believe they do not deserve to be loved by the divine. You are worthy of God's love just because you exist. Your job is to invite this unconditional loving presence into your life; it's that simple. When you invite your God of understanding into your life experience, your life and all life around you gets easier and much more graceful.

However, when you do not invite a power greater than yourself to interact in your life, this choice diminishes your full expression into the world. If you reach into the world without inviting this power in and believing that you do not need help, you will struggle through life. This choice creates an awkwardly clumsy life, a life full of conflict between the ego and the light.

I have heard many people share their stories of times in their lives that they chose this "independent" life style, full of ego (edging God out). For awhile it seemed to be working, then eventually there came a time when God needed to get their attention. And, sometimes the only way for God to get their attention is to change their independent thinking by literally knocking them out of commission.

I know for myself that the biggest spiritual lessons have come to me when I was either sick, hurt, or in the hospital, someone died; I got into a car accident; my back went out, or I was on the edge waiting to get lab results back from some mysterious illness I believed I was harboring. Yes, I used to be very "bull headed" and apparently needed to learn the hard way. But you do not need to learn the hard way if you invite God's love into your life. Invite divine guidance to support you, and then be willing to spiritually listen to the divine whispers within you. Act with your life for the greater, higher good of all, and then there should be no need to "knock you out of commission."

Oprah Winfrey says that the universe speaks to us first in a whisper. Those whispers sound like, "Hmm, that feels odd, or "Hmm, that doesn't make sense," or "Hmm, something just doesn't feel right about this situation." If the whispers don't get your attention then the universe will give you a thump upside the head. Those thumps come as getting a speeding ticket, getting written up at work, having a paid service cut off for non-payment, breaking a body part, blowing out your back and various other possibilities.

If you do not listen to the thumps then the universe has to come in with bigger wake up calls. Those big wake-up calls can come in many forms as well, but they all come with one thing in common – A Huge Mess! In other words, the walls come tumbling down and you are forced into dealing with it. The entire time the universe has been nudging and smacking in all types of ways, we, you, all of us were just not listening. And as Rumi writes, "You can either let go or be dragged!"[24]

God sees more than you can see. God knows more than you know, so to argue with God. I think, we all know that is an undermining process. God, who is the Divine eye in the sky, does see all: the past, the present and the future. The Divine will not take you or anyone anywhere that does not serve the greater, higher good of all. Everything does have a reason, and a spiritually reliable person understands that there is no wrong path. Every path leads you to the exact perfect place, in the exact perfect time and this *time* is Divine timing.

The biggest question I hear in my life's work when teaching around the subject of Spiritual Lessons is:

Why do bad things happen to good people?

I often hear, "How is there a spiritual lesson in an entire family being murdered in their sleep? What type of lesson could there be to a drunk driver killing my sister? What is the spiritual lesson to my dad dying in 9/11?"

I must tell you that these are the hardest questions for me to understand myself. However, this is my truth: our souls are currently living as human beings, living in the physical world. In this world we must understand that the concept of God is beyond our human intellectual capacity. We are not to know these truths yet. We have adapted to live in this reality and God is in every reality, even realities of which we are not aware. We are not privy to the other world's information because it is not needed in our current soul's reality.

You are guided by an unseen presence that is always moving though you, and all around you. This unseen, always-present guide sees everything, or is at least a traveler between the veils of reality. I call this presence God because God is in everything. However, anything you call it should always be of the light. Understand that good exists in everything that was once of light energy. When bad things happen to good people, we will not always understand and sometimes we may never find the answer. But, while in this container we call a human being, we must eventually come to the realization that even in "this," God is. When you come to comprehend this, your life, your mind, your heart will open up and receive. In fact, this may be one of the many reasons we are here to experience life: the lesson of seeing light in all things.

A spiritually reliable person lives with a knowing that there exists far more light energy in the world than dark. They know the truth that there is more love in the world than there is hate. They know the truth that the light will always wash out the dark. They know the bigger truth that there is always a spiritual lesson behind the darkness. As Terry Pratchett writes, "Light thinks it travels faster than anything but it is wrong. No matter how fast light travels, it finds the darkness has always got there first, and is waiting for it."[25]

A spiritually reliable person knows to bring forth the light and truth to every experience; good or bad, and knows that the darkness hides, and to expose it we must bring the truth, the light and the love. When you do, you transcend into a higher vibrational vessel and then you intermingle in the other worlds. The key to the kingdom is "Light and Love".

Many people resist seeing the spiritual lessons in bad things. And if you are someone who struggles with seeing the spiritual lessons, I invite you to ponder these thoughts: A spiritually reliable person reframes from labeling experiences as bad or good? They see all experiences as a "SO?" So it is, it is what it is, this is what I am being served up, so it must have something to teach me, bring to me, show me? Can you see yourself living a life of proactive surrender? To proactively seek to find the spiritual lessons in all those experiences you could label as bad or good? And, to surrender to divine understanding that there are things you just will never understand in this human experience?

It is not always wise or right to expect yourself to find the spiritual lessons right away after you experience something labeled as "bad" in your life. These processes take time, and most are messy and usually painful. Some days you cope better than others; then other days you are barely holding on with hope. You find yourself angry with God one moment and then begging and praying to the same presence that you were just mad at minutes ago. It is a roller coaster of emotions and they are always predictably unpredictable. Emotions are moving targets and to pin them down into a label will eventually not serve you anymore. Emotions need to move and shift; this is natural and it is the process that moves them through you.

Many people do not want to feel their emotions because "feeling" bad is not acceptable in the world. We live in a society that has an atrocious misconception of believing we should always feel good, joy and happy. So, instead of feeling the emotions and seeing these feelings as your greatest wisest teachers, we dim them down with mood stabilizers that repress the feeling, especially if it is a bad feeling.

Look at it this way: When your body is presenting pain, this pain is alerting you that something may be wrong, or malfunctioning. It is like a gauge on the instrument panel of your car. If a gauge lights up, it's alerting you that something may be wrong in the inner workings of the vehicle. When this occurs, it usually catches your attention and you take action in order to prevent the vehicle from getting worse. The same concept should be followed with your body.

As you now know pain in the body can present itself as emotional; it is not meant to be limited to just physical. To find the spiritual lessons in your painful experiences you have to embrace the feelings you are having. In order to heal you must feel, and this is where the real work begins within yourself, in the feelings. You will need to bear down, learn to push through it, ask for revelation, resolution, and resurrection. It is then, and with divine guidance, that you will spend more time in your understanding and acceptance of the spiritual lessons and less in your pain.

Are you ready to transcend, evolve beyond the pain and receive the spiritual lessons? If so, I invite you to integrate these three grounding mantras into your daily life and begin to evoke the spiritual lessons.

Revelation: Revelation is the revealing or disclosing of some form of truth or knowledge through communication with a deity or other supernatural entity or entities.

"Dear God,
I invite the angels of clarity into my experience now so I may see the truth (of/about)
_____. *I know that what I bring to the alter will be altered; therefore, I release this inner struggle to you now. I surrender into the arms of divine knowledge. I allow it to reveal its truth to me in divine order and divine timing. I now claim the truth to be revealed and the spiritual lesson to expose itself to me now. I release this into the Law of God as done. And, so it is."*

Resolution: Analyzing a complex notion into simpler ones, answering or solving. Metaphorically it is to achieve greater resolution; therefore, to see more clearly. It is to transcend the pain and move into the Divine light of God, have an " A Ha" and become aware, awake and divinely realized.

"Dear God,
I am now willing to see the spiritual lesson
clearly and I release any confusion to you. I
accept my human limitations to not always know
the answers and I believe in divine order in all
experiences. I release my attachment to labeling
any experience as bad or good. I know that even
in this, the light of God is present. I may not fully
see the light as clearly as you do, but I am
willing to accept my humanness and to release
the need to know everything to the Divine. I
release this into the Law of God as done. And,
so it is."

Resurrection: Is the concept of a living
being coming back to life after death. In this
meaning we can define resurrection as seeing
the spiritual lessons in shocking events or
experiences as possible, and when we do we are
resurrected. The resurrection can be a death-
defying experience to our souls and our belief in
a moral higher power. In order to be resurrected
from such a soul shifting experience we first
must die to our mortal selves, and then
"resurrect" into our soulful selves. Meaning, we
(our souls) understand that we never end, even
in body death; our souls are eternal energy that
will always be expressing itself into something
throughout eternity. To resurrect is to have this
truth, live this truth, and to know it as everyone's
truth; know it is a part of our life cycle; it is not
wrong or bad. It is just what it is supposed to
be—it is the cycle of life.

Grounding Prayer

Dear God,
I am very clear that from my imprecise vantage
point here on earth, I will never understand all
that you can see. I understand this life is a
temporary teaching phase of my spiritual
experiences. I know that my life, and all life is
eternal and never ends and is expressing itself
through all things. Therefore, I now understand
that when I die to my ego self, the part of me
that believes this is the only experience that
exists. I will then truly resurrect from this
tethered, restricted body in which my ego self
believes is the only dimension. I let go of my
need to know information in which my mental
mind is not prepared to integrate as I walk in my
humanness. I release this into the Law of God
as done. And, so it is.

Chapter 14: Embracing Duality

Your darkness is your greatest and wisest teacher.

du-al-i-ty (noun) 1. Something consisting of two parts—a situation or nature that has two states or parts that are complementary or opposed to each other.[26]

Another way you can labor against living a spiritually reliable life is when you do not embrace your dualities. Duality exists in every person and when you do not embrace that which exists within, you will not reap the effects. You'll come to realize that these parts you ignore will be squashed and covered in shame, which will continue to grow. When you cover anything with a shame blanket its growth will accelerate as negativity; all negativity has a plan to derail you. The only way to take away its drive to thwart you is to wrap it up in words, expose it, and shine a light on it.

When you invite your challenges, problems and your dualities in for a visit (for an interview) you automatically shine a light on them, exposing them and turn them towards the light. Many people equate the word "duality" as bad, dark or wrong, and we must address this idea because our darkest parts and pieces of us are our greatest and wisest teachers. This causes most people do their best to keep these parts "squashed" down when they are in the world.

My prayer for anyone reading this book is to realize that there is no need to judge others; every person has secrets and every person has parts of themselves they would rather not have flashed over the big screen at the ball game. If everyone has dualities, everyone has secrets. Everyone has hands, arms and toes, why would you feel it necessary to hide, conceal and bury them?

Have you ever heard the phrase, "Angel on one shoulder and the devil on the other?" Many clients and students have honestly shared their own dualities of their lives with me in my classes and sessions. What I know is that we all have dualities we carry within us:

- The good and the bad
- The light and the dark
- The love and the trouble
- The faith and the fear
- The wholeness and the shattered
- The enlightenment and the addiction
- The Baptist and the Jew
- The peaceful and the angry
- The happy and the sad
- The in-control and out-of-control
- The aware and the unaware
- The light and the dark
- The confident and the unconfident
- The rich mentality and the poor mentality
- The balanced and the unbalanced

- The mature and the immature
- The open and the closed off
- The brave and the scared
- The passive and the aggressive
- The stable and the unstable
- The deserving and the undeserving
- The creative and the uncreative
- The believer and the non-believer
- The too big and the too little
- The lazy and the over achiever
- The old school and the modern
- The scared and the silly
- The God and the void

This list could go on and on and it's likely you have already individualized it to be more fitting for yourself. I invite you to make a list of your dualities if you wish to gain more insight.

A client scheduled a session with me. I asked her what she would like to work on today. She replied with, "I am not where I am supposed to be in my life. Sometimes I feel enlightened and sometimes I feel like a total mess. Shouldn't I be further along in my process of enlightenment than I am? Some days I feel like I am really on a path of self-awareness --moving forward in a positive direction and suddenly I will find myself off-path and going in a whole different direction. It is like I am on a positive path, and before I know it I am on a negative path, and I am sick and tired of the roller coaster! When is this going to stop so I can always be in a state of awareness and high enlightenment?"

I started laughing out loud–clarifying to the client "I am not laughing at you but with you."

I asked the client if she believes we ever reach total awareness and enlightenment in our lives. She replied with, "Well, Yes of course we do, isn't that what we are all striving to do"?

I replied, "Is it?"

In his book, "Still Here," Ram Dass talks about the Ego versus the Soul. He says the soul needs the ego's lessons to learn and reach Heaven or to enter into union with the Divine—a union of far more spacious context. [27]

If we do not know what dark is we will never understand light; if we do not know what hot is we will never understand cold; if we do not know what fear is we will never understand peace. Or, how do we describe cobalt blue if we have never seen it? It is not actually blue or purple but a mixture of both—sort of... it is just cobalt, and until you see it, you really cannot describe it. If our soul needs the lessons of the ego, which I see as the duality of everyone's personality, then why do we continue to always try to eliminate these parts of us that could be our greatest teacher? Isn't the key to embrace the dualities within us... see them, expose them, understand them and then manage them as great wise teachers who have come to teach us our greatest life lessons?

I do not believe we ever become fully

enlightened beings as long as we are living this human experience. This is what life is about—learning and realizing we are still here because we have lessons to learn and to teach others. We teach what we need to learn the most, and when we are done learning our lessons we will be transported to another level of existence. Until then we are to do our very best to embrace all parts of us. When I say embrace them I do not mean that you should taunt them. Instead take them for a ride by asking them to dance in the mystery and say something like:

Duality (Name it) I am not sure why you are here, presenting yourself as (name it) but I am now ready to explore your life force, which lives within me. I am willing now to sit down, internally, outwardly or through written word and interview you as my greatest and wisest teacher. I am willing to let myself be vulnerable, to get honest and make friends with you.

What are you here to teach me?

What gifts do you bring me?

Something miraculous begins to happen when I have invited these parts of myself that are causing issues in my life in for an interview. When you call it up and out and wrap it up in words, just the process of doing so begins to move the shame energy. This movement will ultimately do one of three things:

1) Move the energy around, scramble it up and turn it into something new.

2) Move it right out of your body, releasing it by the mere exposure.

3) Piss it off, make it mad – but you are still moving energy.

What you must understand in a metaphoric way is that monsters hide in the dark. As long as they stay in the dark they can continue to grow bigger because when we cannot see something our imagination usually makes it bigger than it really is. It is like the scary horror movie we all have watched. The scariest parts are when we hear the music escalate and we know something is about to happen. We cover our eyes, hold our breath and peek through our fingers anticipating what is about to jump out and get us. But, as soon as it finally jumps out and reveals itself, we usually say, "Oh man, really? That wasn't so bad." We almost get bothered with the director of the film for making it feel real and scary.

You are the director of your movie and your movie is full of scary moments, dark moments, joyful moments – all sorts of moments. These moments are never as bad as we perceive them in our own imagination. Human beings are meaning-making machines and this is what sets us apart from the rest of the animal kingdom. We have the tendency to over process our life stuff, and when we do not move it out of our bodies using the power of words, sharing our darkness in a safe place, it can high jack us and spin us for the worst. Once we expose it, process it and move its' energy around, its' power is purged out of us, and we begin to make friends with our duality, making room for right choices. It is only then that our duality does not have the power to derail us; instead we become self-compassionate, free of our shame and harmoniously balanced through the magical power of exposure.

When you expose the things you are hiding, you take the power out of them. Conversely, when you hide these things you cover them up in shame, layer-by-layer, deeper and thicker, year-by-year, until no light can get in, and then eventually you drown in your misunderstood, unexpressed dualities. After years of shoveling shameful baggage over your darkest pieces and parts, and the years of a love-hate relationship take their toll, the only thing left for some of us to do is to die with a belief that we were wrong for acting in these ways, which causes the biggest sin of all in life— *separation.* All problems come from separation. We must address the unhealthy belief that we are not worthy of a relationship with our creator. These beliefs, those thoughts of separation cause, create, and generate more shame, more layers, and less light. Therefore, the solution comes in the name of connection and exposure.

A spiritually reliable vessel is willing to

hold the space for others to process energy. A spiritually reliable vessel seeks for those who will hold space for them as well. They hold a container called empathy. Empathy is showing up for others as neutral—Clear, Available and Ready—being a CAR. Empathy is the ability to understand and share the feelings of another. It does not mean that you have had the same experience in order to completely understand. It means you only need to hold a neutral, safe, mutually respectful space for someone to be heard and seen at their deepest level. When you hold this type of empathy the mystics begin to dance, and the darkness that covers the shame runs in the name of words.

The late Debbie Ford did her best piece of work when she wrote the book, *Shadow Effect*.[28]

She exposed the truth about the real world and that the real world is full of duality. Just because we have learned that it is not cool to be vulnerable and expose our duality and that we must show up as perfect – doesn't mean duality doesn't exist! The more we push it down, hold it down, shove it down – we eventually implode and crack in half. The only solution is to get honest with someone in your life who deserves, and who has earned, the right to "hold this for you." If you do not have this person in your life, then you may want to seek out a professional who can hold the exposure process for you.

Dualities exist in all humans, all colors, all races, all zip codes and in every hierarchy. The one thing I know to be true about all people is that we are all doing the best we can with the resources we have available. And sometimes those resources have come in the form of wearing protective masks – the mask of perfection.

A spiritually reliable person surrounds themselves with other like-minded people who are willing to love, accept and support their process in an unconditional, mutually respectful way. They accept the person and invite the person to change the behavior. They know once committed, the entire universe supports you. They know there are no accidents; only lessons. They know all judgments are self-judgments and they know all problems come from separation; therefore, the solution comes from connection.

I used to teach a class on Diversity and in one of my lessons I would hand out a piece of plain white paper. On one side, on the very top of the page it said:

**I believe most people in the world
see me as....**

And on the other side of the page it said:

What people do not know about me is...

I gave the verbal assignment to expose both sides of them and they are not to write their name on the paper and they must use blue or black ink. I invited them to be brutally honest and write whatever they wanted on both sides of their paper—no one will know it is your paper, your dualities.

Once you are finished, do not fold it or put marks on the paper and then place it in the large box in the middle of the room.

After every student placed his or her mask unveiling in the box, I closed the box tightly, and vigorously shook it – making sure every piece of paper was scrambled around. I reopened the box and went around the room presenting the box to each student giving them the instructions to take one piece of paper from the box and hold it to their chest. I then instructed the students to read one at a time, out loud, starting with the outside mask:

I believe most people in the world see me as....

And then turn the page over and read:

What people do not know about me is...

You are probably thinking to yourself, as you read this, how uncomfortable the students must feel. It is extremely uncomfortable, but as I teach:

When you are uncomfortable it only means you are growing.

What I have witnessed during these "exposure" exercises is beyond uncomfortable.

From the moment the first student begins to read someone else's dualities, the entire room is silent, and you can hear the clock's fast hand ticking away on the wall, the breaths of the students, and everyone is wondering when theirs will be read. These are moments I refer to as "knothole" moments.

A knothole moment is when you're being squeezed through something so tight, so intense, that it becomes a defining, pivotal paradigm shift—shifting your life trajectory into a whole new cosmos.

As each student reads another exposure sheet out loud something magical begins to happen. The sheer act of wrapping these thoughts around words shifts the energy of the room. Connection begins immediately with the very first word read, the courageous act of writing down your inner thoughts and shame, and then placing them into a box for all to hear. This in turn exposes the layers of shame to the light and gives them birth as it lifts them up and right out of you! When you witness others' vulnerabilities, a common thread is woven through all, sewing the room up as one.

Exposure is the idea that monsters hide in the dark, and in order for you to take the power out of the monster you must be willing to shine a light on it. When you expose something that is hiding it becomes powerless.

A spiritually reliable person seeks to shine the light in all areas where there is darkness. Where there is darkness, there is light, and when we seek to see the light in all things, all conditions, all experiences, you will find life is full of duality – the dark and the light. When you make friends with this truth about you and all things, your life, the struggle, the clash and swordfight with duality will magically diminish.

I invite you to **expose** your duality(s) on a separate personal page. It's a simple, miraculous process.

1. Get a note pad or writing tablet and pen or pencil, or create a document on your computer.
2. On the top portion of the page write: **I believe most people in the world see me as...**
3. Turn the page over, and on top of the page write: **What people do not know about me is...**
4. Write everything you want without editing or worrying about spelling. Once you are done, comfortable, and are willing, seek to find someone that you feel has earned the right to witness and hold the container for your full exposure. Ask for what you need, and let the power of exposure free you.

Remember: You are shining a light into the monster's face and taking away its power by wrapping it up in words. Giving it birth to move, change and release the shame blanket that has been suffocating your life force from expressing itself into the world as a spiritually reliable vessel.

Grounding Prayer

Dear God,
I now choose to see all parts and pieces of myself as my greatest and wisest teachers. I call my dualities up and out, and in for an interview through the power of words and writing. I understand that they disclose mighty secrets, and teach me what I need to know next. I let go of all self-judgment and seek to create safe connections with liked minded souls who desire real, honest, deep, unconditional, loving and vulnerable relationships. When I feel safe and supported; I become the fullest and highest expression of my divine self. I know this to be true now. I release this into the Law of God as Done. And, so it is!

About the Author

Richard Seaman is an award winning teacher, speaker and writer. He is the founder and director of Seattle Life Coach Training (SLCT), and one of the nation's top spiritual authors.

A native of Seattle, Richard trains you to transform lives by teaching, training and certifying successful life coaches. He has been a Master Life Coach, Spiritual Leader and Motivational Speaker for more than two decades. With his wise and intuitive knowing, and uplifting and straightforward approach, he has coached and guided thousands of people to a more powerful, passionate life. He continues to grow a very successful Life Coach training program in Seattle, WA.

Richard also teaches at the Southwest Institute of Healing Arts (SWIHA), Arizona's award winning, private holistic healthcare college.

Richard was awarded "Best Teacher of the Year 2011" by the Arizona Private School Association.

Richard is the author of the books: *It's All in the Sharing and It's All in the Sharing—Companion Journal. Spiritual Reliability,* helped secure a spot for Richard as one of America's Next top spiritual authors.

Epilogue: Daniel's Gloves[29]
(cont'd)

'I'll be there!' was my reply. He began his journey again. He headed away with his sign dangling from his bedroll and pack of Bibles. He stopped, turned and said, 'When you see something that makes you think of me, will you pray for me?' 'You bet,' I shouted back, 'God bless.' 'God bless.' And that was the last I saw of him. Late that evening as I left my office, the wind blew strong. The cold front had settled hard upon the town. I bundled up and hurried to my car. As I sat back and reached for the emergency brake, I saw them... a pair of well-worn brown work gloves neatly laid over the length of the handle. I picked them up and thought of my friend and wondered if his hands would stay warm that night without them. Then I remembered his words: 'If you see something that makes you think of me, will you pray for me?' Today his gloves lie on my desk in my office. They help me to see the world and its people in a new way, and they help me remember those two hours with my unique friend and to pray for his ministry. 'See you in the New Jerusalem,' he said. Yes, Daniel, I know I will...

"I shall pass this way but once. Therefore, any good that I can do or any kindness that I can show, let me do it now, for I shall not pass this way again."

We are all conduits for Spirit to utilize us for the greater higher purpose. Daniel's story is an extreme demonstration of being Spiritually Reliable but it is the path onto which he was called.

If you had a path, an assignment, a curriculum to teach—what would it be? Where in your life can you see the opportunity's to be Spiritually Reliable and to be utilized for the greater higher purpose?

If God were an employer would he hire you?

In Divine Timing –

Richard Seaman

Afterword

As a writer who is writing a book you never really know when the book is done, especially a writer who is Spiritually Reliable and only writes when He is inspired to write.

"Inspired" meaning In Spirit, knowing the Spirit of God is moving through me and utilizing my hands and voice for a greater higher purpose. My readers and students ask me all the time how I do it? I always reply with the same answer, which is, "I wait on the whispers within me to guide me and ride me into the next chapter. I wait to feel the spiritual spot, which is a groove I slide into and it lifts me up and over the struggle. My writing then feels inspired, peaceful and full of ease and grace.

This is my second book I have written and when I was writing *It's All in the Sharing* I didn't know when I was done until I basically collapsed from the marathon I had just ran as a writer. The long, intense days and nights I would endure struggling with two components:

1)   I was developing my writing skills and typing skills all at the same time.
2)   I was listening to the God voice within me, the whispers guiding me to write and what to write.

Let's just say, it was quite the dance between God and this human being. There were so many times I would get frustrated and want to give up. Some days my typing was so bad it would hurt to think I was a writer, and some days God was downloading so much information into me I couldn't keep up. Some days I would be in total bliss and completely loose track of time. It felt like something else took over and utilized my body. For those of you who think the Spirit of God isn't demanding I have to correct you and tell you the presence of G.U.S can be laborious. It is absolute hard work and dedication like I have never experienced before. There is no time and space where "Spirit" lives, therefore 4:00 a.m. wake up calls are not uncommon. I hear new chapters and classes in my dreams, late at night, while driving down the road in my car, in the shower, when I watch television, when going to dinner with friends, during random conversations, billboards with messages on them, during church service, teaching classes and even when I may be having arguments with my loved ones. To be *Spiritually Reliable* it takes dedication, follow-through and commitment to be the observer and listener on my many different levels. We have to be multi-dimensional, multi-tasking, multi-sensory and able to dance, listen, walk, talk, teach, help, see, feel and type all at the same time. Are you being *Spiritually Reliable*? I had to throw that in there—well, are you?

In the preface of this book I write the following:

"This time is different because I set out to write a book, which means I have to be spiritually reliable and commit to it's final outcome. I have to show up like it was a job that I have been hired to do.

My writing conveys how to be spiritually reliable. I move in and out of spiritual reliability myself at times, which takes me back to a teaching I teach, 'we teach what we need to learn the most'. Sometimes it is not easy to show up for God to be his hands and voice. Then other times it can be very easy to show up because there is a groove we slide into and somehow it lifts us up, over it and through the struggle connecting to God and becoming Spirit's tool. This space of possibility is a mystery to me everyday. Why sometimes can we find the "groove" and why sometimes do we miss it?"

I have to share with you that I have learned through this journey of writing this book what "Spiritual Reliability" really is. I had an intention, a thought, a goal and an assignment from Spirit to write, edit, create and publish this book. I have been asking for the last few months if I was done? Is this book complete? Can I stop now? Each time I would ask I would sit and wait for the peace to envelope me or hear another message I was supposed to write. Then, last night I was in a half awake-dream state and I heard it was done. I heard today I would make a very important decision. I woke to my normal daily routine of coffee, feeding the dogs and turning on my computer when I received an email that had the last message for the book. This message to me sums up everything I have been trying to convey to my readers. As I read it I was brought to tears because I knew this would be the final chapter. You have by now read the story, *Daniel's* Gloves, which I believe demonstrates true Spiritual Reliability, a story of a man who is braver than possibly you or I. I am not saying this is your journey nor would I suggest it be your journey unless you know it is your path. As you read this story I am sure you related to many parts of it—seeing yourself in either the observer or the devoted Spiritual Reliable doer.

I invite you to walk into your life as a Spiritually Reliably vessel. I invite you to know that each encounter you have is a divine appointment that can serve the greater higher good of all. I invite you to walk with the mindset of a *spiritually reliable* achiever. I invite you to release this as your truth into the Law of God as Done.

If God were an employer would he hire you? I say Yes, You've been hired! And, so it is!

SEATTLE
LIFE COACH TRAINING
train to transform lives

Welcome to Seattle Life Coach Training!

Whether you are interested in embarking on your own journey, or are being called to coach, Seattle Life Coach Training (SLCT) will provide you with the tools and resources you need to change your life, and the lives of those around you. SLCT is a real-time, in-person, residential life coach training program located in Seattle, WA. Our course incorporates a connection to spirituality, intuition, higher power and your own inner knowing. You will receive unparalleled life coach training, find your voice, and show up in the world in a different, more powerful way. Upon completion of the 100-hour life coach-training program you will earn your Life Coaching certification.

Seattle Life Coach Training offers two start dates a year and our lead by Richard Seaman and his trained transformational life-coaching instructors.

SLCT will take you every step of the way as you embark on this intense, exciting transformational approach to becoming a life coach.

train to transform lives

www.SeattleLifeCoachTraining.com

Appendix
Mayo Clinic Article on Forgiveness[30]

What is forgiveness?

Generally, forgiveness is a decision to let go of resentment and thoughts of revenge. The act that hurt or offended you might always remain a part of your life, but forgiveness can lessen its grip on you and help you focus on other, positive parts of your life. Forgiveness can even lead to feelings of understanding, empathy and compassion for the one who hurt you.

Forgiveness doesn't mean that you deny the other person's responsibility for hurting you, and it doesn't minimize or justify the wrong. You can forgive the person without excusing the act. Forgiveness brings a kind of peace that helps you go on with life.

What are the benefits of forgiving someone?

Letting go of grudges and bitterness can make way for compassion, kindness and peace. Forgiveness can lead to:

- Healthier relationships both with others and yourself;
- Greater spiritual and psychological well-being;

- Less anxiety, stress and hostility;
- Lower blood pressure;
- Fewer symptoms of depression;
- Lowers the risk of alcohol and substance abuse.

- ## Why is it so easy to hold a grudge?

When someone you love and trust hurts you, you might become angry, sad or confused. If you dwell on hurtful events or situations, grudges filled with resentment, vengeance and hostility can take root. If you allow negative feelings to crowd out positive feelings, you might find yourself swallowed up by your own bitterness or sense of injustice.

What are the effects of holding a grudge?

If you're unforgiving, you might pay the price repeatedly by bringing anger and bitterness into every relationship and new experience. Your life might become so wrapped up in the wrong that you can't enjoy the present. You might become depressed or anxious. You might feel that your life lacks meaning or purpose, or that you're at odds with your spiritual beliefs. You might lose valuable and enriching connectedness with others.

How do I reach a state of forgiveness?

Forgiveness is a commitment to a process of change. To begin, you might:

- Consider the value of forgiveness and its importance in your life at a given time;
- Reflect on the facts of the situation, how you've reacted, and how this combination has affected your life, health and well—being;
- When you're ready, actively choose to forgive the person who's offended you;
- Move away from your role as victim and release the control and power the offending person and situation have had in your life;

As you let go of grudges, you'll no longer define your life by how you've been hurt. You might even find compassion and understanding.

What happens if I can't forgive someone?

Forgiveness can be challenging, especially if the person who's hurt you doesn't admit wrong or doesn't speak of his or her sorrow. If you find yourself stuck, consider the situation from the other person's point of view. Ask yourself why he or she would behave in such a way. Perhaps you would have reacted similarly if you faced the same situation. In addition, consider broadening your view of the world. Expect occasional imperfections from the people in your life. You might want to reflect on times you've hurt others and on those who've forgiven you. It can also be helpful to write in a journal, pray or use guided meditation—or talk with a person you've found to be wise and compassionate, such as a spiritual leader, a mental health provider, or an impartial loved one or friend.

Does forgiveness guarantee reconciliation?

If the hurtful event involved someone whose relationship you otherwise value, forgiveness can lead to reconciliation. This isn't always the case, however. Reconciliation might be impossible if the offender has died or is unwilling to communicate with you. In other cases, reconciliation might not be appropriate. Still, forgiveness is possible—even if reconciliation isn't.

What if I have to interact with the person who hurt me but I don't want to?

If you haven't reached a state of forgiveness, being near the person who hurt you might be tense and stressful. To handle these situations, remember that you can choose to attend or avoid specific functions and gatherings. Respect yourself and do what seems best. If you choose to attend, don't be surprised by a certain amount of awkwardness and perhaps even more intense feelings. Do your best to keep an open heart and mind. You might find that the experience helps you to move forward with forgiveness.

What if the person I'm forgiving doesn't change?

Getting another person to change his or her actions, behavior or words isn't the point of forgiveness. Think of forgiveness more about how it can change your life—by bringing you peace, happiness, and emotional and spiritual healing. Forgiveness can take away the power the other person continues to wield in your life.

What if I'm the one who needs forgiveness?

The first step is to honestly assess and acknowledge the wrongs you've done and how those wrongs have affected others. At the same time, avoid judging yourself too harshly. You're human, and you'll make mistakes. If you're truly sorry for something you've said or done, consider admitting it to those you've harmed. Speak of your sincere sorrow or regret, and specifically ask for forgiveness—without making excuses. Remember, however, you can't force someone to forgive you. Others need to move to forgiveness in their own time. Whatever the outcome, commit to treating others with compassion, empathy and respect and choose to apply love like you were applying salve to a cut.

Notes

[1] A Course In Miracles—citation

[2] Galatians 5:22 -24: NIV.

[3] Nahmod, Daniel, "One Power," compact disc.

[4] Richard Ryan, "Daniel's Gloves," http://www.sun-crusher.net/DanielsGloves.php.

[5] Lillian Quigley, *The Blind Men and The Elephant*, (New York: Atheneum, 1969).

[6] Esther Hicks and Jerry Hicks, *The Law of Attraction Journal,* http://www.abraham-hicks.com/lawofattractionsource/journal.php?journal_category=8.

[7] Oprah Winfrey, Oprah Winfrey Network, http://www.oprah.com/oprahshow/Country-Superstar-Keith-Urban-Opens-Up-for-the-First-Time/5.

[8] Marianne Williamson, *A Return to Love – Reflections on the Principles of A Course in Miracles,* (New York, NY: HaperCollins, 1993).

[9] *Living the Science of Mind*, (DeVorss & Company, 1984), pg. 434.

[10] citation—Course in Miracles

[11] Ecclesiastes 6:11; NIV.

[12] citation—is the context a part of this quote or your addition? Also, it appears in the meaning that it is not perfectly cited... I saw this before. We need to make sure it is exactly as Webster has it.

[13] Citation – A Course in Miracles

[14] Marianne Williamson, *A Return to Love – Reflections on the Principles of A Course in Miracles* . (New York, NY: HaperCollins 1993), pg. 308. –need to check for accuracy.

[15] Newton-John, Olivia. *Instrument Of Peace.*
        Label: ONJ Productions, Inc., October 3, 2006.

[16] Marianne Williamson, *A Return to Love – Reflections on the Principles of A Course in Miracles* . (New York, NY: HaperCollins 1993), pg. 308. –need to check for accuracy.

[17] Mayo Clinic Staff, "Forgiveness: Letting go of grudges and bitterness." http://www.mayoclinic.org/forgiveness/art-20047692.

[18] Ibid.

[19] citation - *A Course in Miracles*

[20] Mathew 7:7;NIV.

[21] *The Horse Whisperer*, directed by Robert Redford (1998; Burbank, CA: Touchstone Home Video, 1998), DVD.

[22] T.S. Eliot, "Little Gidding." http://www.columbia.edu/itc/history/winter/w3 206/edit/tseliotlittlegidding.html

[23] Louise Hay, *The Power Is Within You*, (Carlsbad, CA: Hay House, 1991).

[24] Rumi, Jalal ad-Din Muhammad . Open to Wellness, "Two Most Important Steps In Wellness – #1 Be Willing To Change", http://opentowellnessblog.com/two-most-important-steps-in-wellness-1-be-willing-to-change/   find a more original source

[25] Terry Pratchett, Good Reads, "Terry Pratchett, Quotable Quotes," http://www.goodreads.com/quotes/42499-light-thinks-it-travels-faster-than-anything-but-it-is find a more original source

[27] Ram Dass, *Still Here: Embracing Aging, Changing and Dying*, (U.S.A: Riverhead Books, 2001).

[28] Deepak Chopra, Debbie Ford, and Marianne Williamson, *The Shadow Effect: Illuminating the True Power of Your Hidden Self,* (NewYork: Harper One, 2010).

[29] Ibid.

[30] Mayo Clinic Staff, "Forgiveness: Letting go of grudges and bitterness." http://www.mayoclinic.org/forgiveness/art-20047692.

Bibliography

Bible: NEW INTERNATIONAL VERSION.

Chopra, Deepak, Ford, Debbie, and
    Williamson, Marianne. *The
    Shadow Effect: Illuminating the True
    Power of Your Hidden
    Self.* NewYork: Harper One, 2010.

Dass, Ram. *Still Here: Embracing Aging,
    Changing, and Dying.* U.S.A.: Riverhead
    Books, June 1, 2001.

Eliot, T.S. Columbia University, "Little
    Gidding." Accessed March
    19, 2014.
    http://www.columbia.edu/itc/history/wint
    er/w3206/edit/tseliotlittlegidding.html.

Hay, Louise. *The Power Is Within You.*
    Carlsbad, CA: Hay House,
    1991.

Hicks, Esther and Jerry. *The Law of
    Attraction: The Basics of the
    Teachings of Abraham.* Hay House,
    September 25, 2006.

Holmes, Ernest. *Living the Science of Mind,*
    (DeVorss & Company, 1984), pg. 434.

Mayo Clinic Staff, "Forgiveness: Letting go of grudges and bitterness." Last modified November 23, 2011. Accessed March 19, 2014. http://www.mayoclinic.org/forgiveness/art-20047692

Mester, Ben. http://article-dashboard.com/Article/TheAge-of-Communication/57067

Nahmod, Daniel. *One Power*. CD Baby, July 8, 2002. http://www.danielnahmod.com.

Newton-John, Olivia. *Instrument Of Peace*. Label: ONJ Productions, Inc., October 3, 2006.

Pratchett, Terry. Good Reads, "Terry Pratchett, Quotable Quotes." Accessed March 19, 2014. http://www.goodreads.com/quotes/42499-light-thinks-it-travels-faster-than-anything-but-it-is.

Quigley, Lillian. *The Blind Men and The Elephant*. New york: Atheneum , 1969.

Ryan, Richard. Sun-Crusher.net: Spreading

the Good News, "Daniel's Gloves."
Accessed March 19, 2014.
http://www.sun-
crusher.net/DanielsGloves.php.

Rumi, Jalal ad-Din Muhammad . Open to
Wellness, "Two Most Important
Steps In Wellness – #1 Be Willing To
Change". Accessed March 19, 2014.
http://opentowellnessblog.com/two-most-
important-steps-in-wellness-1-be-willing-to-
change/

Schucman, H. and Wapnick, K. *A Course in
Miracles* **unknown version.**

The Horse Whisperer, directed by Robert
Redford (1998; Burbank,
CA: Touchstone Home Video, 1998), DVD.

Williamson, Marianne. *A Return to Love –
Reflections on the Principles of A Course
in Miracles* . New York, NY: HaperCollins,
pg. 308, 1993.

Winfrey, Oprah. Oprah Winfrey Network,
Accessed March 19, 2014.
http://www.oprah.com/oprahshow/County-
Superstar-Keith-Urban- Opens-Up-for-the-First-
Time/5.

Winfrey, Oprah. *Super Soul Sunday*. Oprah
    Winfrey Network. Web,
    http://myown.oprah.com/search/index.ht
    ml?own_only=1&q=super soul sunday.*

Note: Some of the content from this book was revised and pulled from Oprah Winfrey's *Super Soul Sunday* featuring exclusive interviews and conversations between **Oprah Winfrey** and top thinkers, authors, filmmakers and spiritual leaders.